P9-CAO-175

**New Directions for
Institutional Research**

Robert K. Toutkoushian
EDITOR-IN-CHIEF

J. Fredericks Volkwein
Paul D. Umbach
ASSOCIATE EDITORS

Data-Driven Decision Making in Intercollegiate Athletics

Jennifer Lee Hoffman
James Soto Antony
Daisy D. Alfaro
EDITORS

Number 144 • Winter 2009
Jossey-Bass
San Francisco

DATA-DRIVEN DECISION MAKING IN INTERCOLLEGIATE ATHLETICS
Jennifer Lee Hoffman, James Soto Antony, Daisy D. Alfaro (eds.)
New Directions for Institutional Research, no. 144
Robert K. Toutkoushian, Editor-in-Chief

NEW DIRECTIONS FOR INSTITUTIONAL RESEARCH (ISSN 0271-0579, electronic ISSN 1536-075X) is part of The Jossey-Bass Higher and Adult Education Series and is published quarterly by Wiley Subscription Services, Inc., A Wiley Company, at Jossey-Bass, 989 Market Street, San Francisco, California 94103-1741 (publication number USPS 098-830). Periodicals Postage Paid at San Francisco, California, and at additional mailing offices. POSTMASTER: Send address changes to New Directions for Institutional Research, Jossey-Bass, 989 Market Street, San Francisco, California 94103-1741.

SUBSCRIPTIONS cost $109 for individuals and $264 for institutions, agencies, and libraries in the United States. See order form at end of book.

EDITORIAL CORRESPONDENCE should be sent to Robert K. Toutkoushian, Educational Leadership and Policy Studies, Education 4220, 201 N. Rose Ave., Indiana University, Bloomington, IN 47405.

New Directions for Institutional Research is indexed in *CIJE: Current Index to Journals in Education* (ERIC), *Contents Pages in Education* (T&F), and *Current Abstracts* (EBSCO).

Microfilm copies of issues and chapters are available in 16mm and 35mm, as well as microfiche in 105mm, through University Microfilms, Inc., 300 North Zeeb Road, Ann Arbor, Michigan 48106-1346.

www.josseybass.com

THE ASSOCIATION FOR INSTITUTIONAL RESEARCH was created in 1966 to benefit, assist, and advance research leading to improved understanding, planning, and operation of institutions of higher education. Publication policy is set by its Publications Committee.

For information about the Association for Institutional Research, write to the following address:

AIR Executive Office
1435 E. Piedmont Drive
Suite 211
Tallahassee, FL 32308-7955

(850) 385-4155

air@mailer.fsu.edu
http://airweb.org

CONTENTS

EDITORS' NOTES

Intercollegiate athletics remains an area of higher education that is a data-intensive endeavor by its very nature. In earlier eras, data on intercollegiate athletics were limited to box scores found in the fine print on the last page of the daily newspaper: final scores, wins and losses, and individual player performance statistics. And though these sorts of data remain essential indicators of success on the field of play, demands for more sophisticated academic, fiscal, gender-equity, staffing, and student athlete experience information have moved the realm of data-based decision making into areas off the field.

In 1992, Mallette and Howard edited *Monitoring and Assessing Intercollegiate Athletics* for the New Directions in Institutional Research series. Their volume addressed issues that remain timely and important in higher education. Since then, the availability and importance of data for decision making in intercollegiate athletics have evolved and increased. The Knight Commission on Intercollegiate Athletics, Andrew W. Mellon Foundation, Women's Sports Foundation, and the National Collegiate Athletic Association (NCAA), all collect and report data on college athletics. The federal government, through the Department of Education's Equity in Athletics Disclosure Act (EADA) Cutting Tool Web site, National Center for Educational Statistics, and Government Accountability Office, makes data and reports on college athletics available online. Individual scholars and campus-based research institutes such as the Institute for Diversity and Ethics in Sport, the Project on Women and Social Change at Smith College (previously at Brooklyn College of the City University of New York), and the Higher Education Research Institute, use empirical data and reports to examine the academic progress, hiring trends, gender equity, and aspects of the student athlete experience. News organizations like the *Chronicle of Higher Education* and *USA Today* have created data sources on gender equity and coaching contracts in Division I football.

The first widespread, systematic collection of academic data on athletics began in 1964. At the time, freshmen were not eligible for varsity competition, and high school grades and test scores were used to predict freshman grade point averages for athletic scholarship eligibility. Then in 1986 the NCAA overhauled eligibility standards under Proposition 48 legislation. Later the Student Athlete Right-to-Know Act of 1990 required institutions to report student athlete graduation information by sport, race, and gender for all institutions. The issues and discussions these policies

NEW DIRECTIONS FOR INSTITUTIONAL RESEARCH, no. 144, Winter 2009 © Wiley Periodicals, Inc.
Published online in Wiley InterScience (www.interscience.wiley.com) • DOI: 10.1002/ir.308

prompted have focused attention on the academic preparation and progress of incoming student athletes, fueling demands for empirical information on college athletics. These demands have come from many stakeholders, including the federal government, journalists, and college presidents. Public awareness of the issue has expanded the need for further data.

The breadth and depth of data on college sports have developed into a robust array of institutional and national sources, many of which did not exist when the first *New Directions* volume dedicated to this issue was published. The first volume astutely made the call for better sources of academic progress and outcomes and measures of academic integrity, and it rightly advocated for self-study and accreditation data to inform decision making on intercollegiate athletics. Since the publication of that volume, the role of institutional researchers and their ability to build systems to meet new requests for data to meet the emerging information challenges associated with college athletics have increased.

The first *New Directions* volume on athletics provided a road map for institutional researchers to develop "consistent and valid data information about the academic progress of all students" and how to respond to requests for specific information on student athletes (Mallette and Howard, 1992, p. 3). This volume picks up where the first left off, addressing the growth of information sources and the ease by which data can now be collected, analyzed, and shared. This volume describes the landscape of data that now exist about student athletes and intercollegiate athletics; it pushes the discussion of how the proliferation of data can be used for decision making while highlighting the areas that still need development.

About This Volume

Data-Driven Decision Making in Intercollegiate Athletics will be useful to institutional researchers, campus decision makers, students, and scholars who seek to understand the current landscape of information about intercollegiate athletics. This volume is a practical resource for those who aim to use existing information for decision making, developing new sources of information, or understanding their athletic department better. Its purposes are to introduce readers to the sources of intercollegiate athletics data, illustrate the critical questions and challenges related to these data, and discuss how these data sources can be used to aid decision making throughout the administration and governance of intercollegiate athletics.

In preparing this volume, we sought the advice of college and university presidents, scholars in higher education and athletic administration, athletic conference commissioners, and athletic directors across the nation. We asked these colleagues about how data inform decision making in intercollegiate athletics today. From them we learned about what data are available and what data have the greatest impact on everyday decisions.

NEW DIRECTIONS FOR INSTITUTIONAL RESEARCH • DOI: 10.1002/ir

When it comes to decision making, we heard from our colleagues that academic and financial issues dominate the landscape of data and feature prominently in decisions about sport sponsorship, facilities, member category, and gender equity, particularly at institutions that have large Division I athletic programs. Growth in the quality and availability of academic and fiscal data has stimulated the creation of new data management systems that aid decision making, such as the NCAA's Dashboard Indicators Project.

And although finances are at the forefront of many policy decisions, other data sources and information about gender equity and student engagement with college pursuits are receiving increased attention. Awareness is growing on the utility of longitudinal reporting about who is hired in staffing and coaching vacancies and who is in a position to make these decisions. We also know much more about the perception faculty members have of athletics and their interest in participating in campus-level athletics decisions. Through the College Sports Project, research on educational outcomes among Division III athletic programs, presidents can view a variety of measures that constitute institution-specific and peer-level comparison data about student athletes. Finally, the NCAA has been collecting large-scale longitudinal data on injuries since 1982, informing rules changes that promote a healthy, safe athletic environment for students.

This volume reflects many of these new data projects and initiatives, describing, chapter by chapter, how these data sources look and can be used. This volume represents a series of chapters that might be loosely organized around four themes: finance and decision making, participation in athletics, academics and athletics, and decision making in athletics.

With respect to finance and decision making, Frank Hodge and Lloyd Tanlu in Chapter One walk readers through various forms of the budgeting process and how it can drive good decision making in college athletics. In Chapter Two, Welch Suggs looks at the history of intercollegiate athletics fiscal data and shows how organizations, initiatives, and reform efforts have evolved in ways that have fundamentally shaped the types of data available today.

On the topic of participation in college athletics, Joy Gaston Gayles, in Chapter Three, discusses data sources available for studying the experience of student athletes on college campuses and highlights the need for national-level data to address complex questions concerning this population. Among the greatest changes since the 1992 volume are the attention paid to gender equity and the use of participation data in institutional decision making. Athena Yiamouyiannis describes these data in Chapter Four by presenting and discussing the use of NCAA and EADA data. Data on the well-being of student athletes participating in college athletics are addressed in Chapter Five by David Klossner, Jill Corlette, Julie Agel, and Stephen W. Marshall. These authors discuss how the health and welfare of student athletes can be addressed using the NCAA Injury Surveillance System and show how sport injury and exposure data have been used to enable policy-makers to make data-driven decisions on policy, rules, and equipment.

The theme of academics and athletics is touched on first in Chapter Six by John Emerson, Rachelle L. Brooks, and Elaine Croft McKenzie. They show data from the national College Sports Project and illustrate the impact of participation in athletics on student athletes' academic performance. Also among the biggest changes since the first volume has been in the areas of academic performance data. Todd A. Petr and Thomas S. Paskus in Chapter Seven explain the new measures of academic integrity that have been developed. They describe how the NCAA collects academic data on high school and college student athletes and the national policies that have been framed by these data.

Finally, decision making in athletics ranges from department-level decisions to broader policy decisions from campus and external constituents. C. Keith Harrison, Richard E. Lapchick, and Neza K. Janson describe in Chapter Eight how sport management and higher education scholars discuss access discrimination and the underrepresentation of racial minorities in athletic administration and head coaching positions in college sports, while offering perspectives on how to address this diversity issue. In Chapter Nine, Janet H. Lawrence describes the perspectives of faculty regarding decision making and oversight of intercollegiate athletics at Division I Football Bowl Subdivision institutions and discusses implications for institutional researchers. Daisy D. Alfaro and Jennifer L. Hoffman provide a comprehensive overview of data resources in Chapter Ten that includes a parallel Web site for electronic sources, and glossary of terms used throughout the volume.

Conclusion

The 1992 volume on the topic of intercollegiate athletics noted that the demands for data have always been subjected "to closer scrutiny from a wider set of interested constituencies" and the "demands for documentation about intercollegiate athletics are the platform where colleges are challenged the most to demonstrate the integrity of their academic, as well as athletic, programs and leadership" (Mallette and Howard, 1992, p. 85). Today the situation is no different.

Questions still remain regarding the impact of intercollegiate athletic programs on higher education. A high-profile athletic program is thought to increase the visibility of an institution, primarily by increasing the number of applicants for admission. Growth in spending on football is thought to decrease spending in other parts of the athletic department. A successful athletic program is widely believed to increase alumni engagement, particularly through annual giving. Investing in infrastructure and program operations at a Division II or Football Championship Series program in an effort to "move up" to NCAA Division I Football Bowl Series membership status is thought to increase the visibility of the athletic program and raise the profile of the institution. Yet research demonstrates that these are complex issues, and these assumptions are not universally supported. For example, the impact of a successful athletic program on donations is also related to the academic reputation of the institution (Stinson and Howard, 2007). In addition, increases in spending in the athletic department do not have a universal impact on the quality of applications to the institution (Orszag and Orszag, 2005).

Only empirical evidence stemming from solid data can help test these and other assumptions in the hopes of preparing leaders to make better decisions in college athletics. Institutional researchers at individual colleges or universities, research centers or institutes, and within national bodies such as the NCAA or other associations are well positioned to collect, analyze, and distribute high-quality, intercollegiate athletics-specific data. We believe that when such data are made available to presidents, faculty members, athletic directors, and other stakeholders, a foundation for decisions that align institutional mission and priorities with policy on intercollegiate athletics will have been laid.

Jennifer Lee Hoffman
James Soto Antony
Daisy D. Alfaro
Editors

References

Mallette, B. I., and Howard, R. D. (eds.). *Monitoring and Assessing Intercollegiate Athletics*. New Directions for Institutional Research, no. 74. San Francisco: Jossey-Bass, 1992.

Orszag, J. M., and Orszag, P. R. *The Empirical Effects of Collegiate Athletics: An Update*. National Collegiate Athletic Association, 2005. Retrieved May 4, 2009, from http://www.ncaa.org.

Stinson, J. L., and Howard, D. R. "Athletic Success and Private Giving to Athletic and Academic Programs at NCAA Institutions." *Journal of Sport Management*, 2007, 21(2), 235–264.

JENNIFER LEE HOFFMAN *is a research associate with the Center for Leadership in Athletics at the University of Washington.*

JAMES SOTO ANTONY *is professor in educational leadership and policy, director of the Center for Leadership in Athletics, and associate vice provost and associate dean for academic affairs in the Graduate School at the University of Washington.*

DAISY D. ALFARO *is a doctoral student in the Educational Leadership and Policy Studies Program and research assistant in the Center for Leadership in Athletics at the University of Washington.*

1

This chapter reviews the main sources of financial data on intercollegiate athletics and the budgeting processes used in athletics.

Finances and College Athletics

Frank Hodge, Lloyd Tanlu

In 2008–2009, the National Collegiate Athletic Association (NCAA) generated television and marketing revenues of approximately $591 million, college sports apparel sales topped $4 billion, and several schools signed multimedia-rights deals for more than $100 million (Berkowitz, 2009; National Collegiate Athletic Association, 2009). At the Division I level intercollegiate athletics is big business, and it is becoming more so among Division II, III, and National Association of Intercollegiate Athletics (NAIA) programs. In this environment, the most effective and successful leaders understand the importance of acquiring, analyzing, and using financial information to make informed decisions. This chapter introduces the public sources of financial data on intercollegiate athletics and describes the budgeting process for effective decision making.

Public Sources of Financial Data for Intercollegiate Athletics

A good place to gather information for intercollegiate athletics as a whole is the NCAA. The NCAA's Web site has a link to "budget and finances," which takes readers to information about the NCAA in general as well as information about each division within the NCAA. The charts in Figure 1.1 are from that Web site and show budgeted revenues (inflows) and expenses (outflows) for the NCAA from the beginning of September 2008 to the end of August 2009. (In some instances, revenues are referred to as "sales," and expenses are sometimes referred to as "costs.") Most of the NCAA's

NEW DIRECTIONS FOR INSTITUTIONAL RESEARCH, no. 144, Winter 2009 © Wiley Periodicals, Inc.
Published online in Wiley InterScience (www.interscience.wiley.com) • DOI: 10.1002/ir.309

Figure 1.1. NCAA budgeted revenues and expenses for 2008–2009*

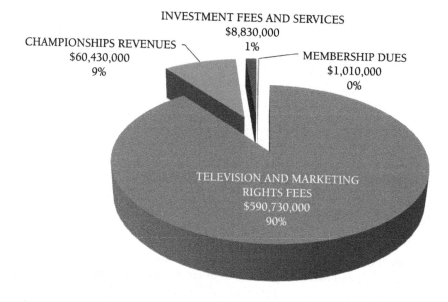

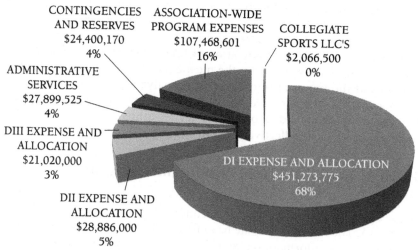

revenue comes from television and marketing rights fees. The $591 million received for such fees in 2008–2009 represents 90 percent of total revenues. The largest expense category for the NCAA is "Division I (DI) expense and allocation," totaling $451 million (68 percent of total expenses). In a more detailed budget provided on the NCAA's Web site, this expense category is broken down into multiple items. The two largest items are "distributions to DI members," totaling $387 million (59 percent of total expenses), and "DI championships and programs," totaling $64 million (10 percent of total expenses). Although the NCAA Web site provides good summary statistics for intercollegiate athletics as a whole, it does not provide institution-specific details.

Financial information related to athletics for most institutions can be found through the U.S. Department of Education's Web site (http://ope.ed .gov/athletics). This Web site provides financial information for postsecondary academic institutions that participate in intercollegiate athletics and in the federal student financial assistance program. Institutions that meet these two criteria must file the Equity in Athletics Disclosure Act (EADA) form with the U.S. Department of Education. This annual filing includes information on athletic participation, coaching staff and salaries, revenues and expenses, and other related information. Much of the information is broken down by gender as well as type of sport (such as football, basketball, and volleyball). The Department of Education's Web site allows users to acquire information on specific institutions or to acquire aggregated information by sorting the data by sanctioning body (including the NCAA and NAIA), state, conference, undergraduate enrollment, or type of institution (four-year, two-year, public, and private, for example). It is important to keep in mind when using these data that not all institutions classify specific revenue and expense items in the same manner, especially prior to 2006. In August 2004, the NCAA updated its "agreed-on procedures" for reporting financial information to more clearly define what institutions should include in specified revenue and expense line items. These new definitions went into effect in early 2006 and reduced, but did not eliminate, discrepancies in the ways that institutions report revenues and expenses.

Finally, in 2008, the NCAA started providing, on a password-protected Web site, what it refers to as "dashboard indicators." Currently there are twenty-six indicators, most of which pertain to financial information. Jim Isch, the chief financial officer at the NCAA, describes the dashboard indicators as "graphic comparisons of the annual financial picture of the institution's athletic program versus a set of comparators" (http://ncaa.org/wps/ ncaa?ContentID=145). Once users select a dashboard indicator, they are shown a graphical presentation of how their institution compares to a predefined (such as by conference) or custom-designed (including individually selected peer institutions) group of institutions on the selected indicator over the previous three years. Currently only a select group of individuals (presidents, athletic directors, and others) have access to the dashboard indicators.

Given this general description of where financial data for intercollegiate athletics can be acquired, we turn our attention to describing the budgeting process and how budgets can be used to make informed decisions.

What Is a Budget?

A *budget* is a projected set of financial consequences based on future plans, goals, and objectives. *Budgeting*, the process by which athletic departments prepare budgets, entails projecting specific revenues and expenses for a given period of time. Each revenue or expense item listed in a budget is commonly referred to as a *line item*.

Two of the most common of the many types of budgets are *capital budgets* and *operating budgets*. A capital budget focuses on large, long-term construction projects, such as a new academic services center or the renovation of an existing stadium. An operating budget focuses on the day-to-day activities of an athletic department, athletic team, or support unit, such as marketing. In this section we focus on operating budgets.

A budget is a useful decision-making tool because it requires administrators and coaches to think about the future and to quantify their expectations. Budgets can be used to guide decisions about everything from how much to pay new or existing coaches, to the implications of cutting specific programs or units. The format and level of detail of a budget vary across institutions and sometimes across programs within an institution. At one extreme, a budget may contain only a limited number of highly aggregated revenue and expense line items. Table 1.1 provides an example of an aggregated budget for a Division I athletic department. At the other extreme, a budget may contain multiple pages of detailed projections of specific revenue and expense line items. To picture a more detailed budget, imagine each line item in Table 1.1 being broken down by sport, such that under the line item "Ticket sales," there would be a line listing the projected dollar amount of ticket sales for each individual sport. On the expense side, a more detailed budget might take a line item like "Travel" and not only break it down by sport, but also by detailed expense category, such as airfare, hotel, and food. Individual administrators and coaches at lower levels within an athletic department are generally responsible for individual line items within an athletic department's overall budget, while more senior administrators assume responsibility for the budget as a whole.

Budgets are often expressed in dollars, but may also include other metrics, such as labor hours, number of personnel, or units (such as the number of footballs needed for spring practice) that help justify the dollar figures. The period covered by a budget is referred to as the *budget horizon* and can vary from a short-term weekly operating budget to a long-term, ten-year capital budget (money for a new stadium, for example). Typically shorter-term budgets are more detailed because there is less uncertainty about expected outcomes one week from today than there is five years from today. This does not mean, however, that short-term budgets are more important than long-term budgets. In fact, in higher education, athletics, or the business world, many argue that success comes from thinking about what will happen to an organization next year, not next week.

NEW DIRECTIONS FOR INSTITUTIONAL RESEARCH • DOI: 10.1002/ir

Table 1.1. Sample Division I Athletic Department Operating Budget, 2009–2010

	2009–2010 Projections	Percentage of Total Revenues
Operating Revenues		
Ticket sales	$10,200,000	26%
Contributions related to season tickets	7,600,000	19
NCAA and conference distributions	6,400,000	16
Multimedia rights	3,600,000	9
Other sponsorships	2,400,000	6
Student fees	6,200,000	15
Concessions, souvenirs, and parking	800,000	2
Investment income	2,000,000	5
Other miscellaneous revenues	800,000	2
Total operating revenues	$40,000,000	100%
Operating expenses		
Salaries and benefits	$16,000,000	40%
Scholarships and financial aid	5,600,000	14
Travel	2,800,000	7
Day of game	2,400,000	6
Guarantees paid to visiting teams	1,600,000	4
Advertising	1,600,000	4
Supplies and equipment	1,200,000	3
Utilities, repairs, and maintenance	3,200,000	8
Other miscellaneous expenses	4,000,000	10
Total operating expenses	$38,400,000	96%
Operating income	$1,600,000	4%

Budgets can be used for planning purposes or performance assessment purposes, or both. It is common in both intercollegiate athletics and the business world to use budgets for both purposes. That is, individuals or departments are asked to create a budget that quantifies their expectations of the future, and then periodically their actual performance is measured against their expected performance. To facilitate the review process, budgets often contain three columns: one that lists the originally forecasted numbers, one that contains actual results, and one that calculates the difference between the two. Understanding the difference between the original forecasted numbers and the actual outcomes is critical to improving the ability to budget accurately over time.

For example, an athletic director might meet with each coach after their respective season ends to review the difference between their team's actual performance and expected (budgeted) performance. If during this review they find that an expense line item ended up being higher than the budgeted amount, they can discuss the reasons why this occurred and whether these reasons are expected to persist. If the reasons are likely to persist (for example, the cost of air travel has increased and is not likely to revert to lower levels in the foreseeable future), future budgets can be appropriately adjusted to reflect these changes.

Preparing Budgets: How Is It Done, and Who Is Involved?

The budgeting process for most athletic departments in general starts with a revenue forecast, since revenue forecasts influence many of the other line items listed in a budget. Revenue forecasts should include projected unit quantities (such as number of tickets sold or number of students) and unit prices whenever possible. After preparing the revenue forecast, administrators and coaches must consider the expenses their respective departments or programs will incur during the period. Some of the expenses will vary with the level of forecasted revenue (for example, the cost of goods sold at concession stands will vary depending on the number of tickets sold). An expense that varies depending on the level of activity is called a *variable expense*. Keeping in mind the revenue forecast when forecasting variable expenses is critical. Other expenses, such as the fixed portion of a coach's salary, will not vary with the level of forecasted revenue. An expense that does not vary depending on the level of activity is called a *fixed expense*.

Preparing a budget can be done in several ways. If the budgeting process involves dialogue between senior administrators and lower-level personnel, it is called *participative*. Many athletic departments use a participative budgeting process because in most cases, lower-level administrators and coaches better understand the individual line items they are responsible for in the athletic department's budget than do more senior administrators. Furthermore, involving lower-level personnel increases the probability that everyone in the athletic department is committed to creating and using budgets to manage their respective departments or programs.

A participative budgeting process usually has several steps. First, senior administrators lay out assumptions that lower-level administrators and coaches use to build their respective budgets. Lower-level personnel then communicate their preliminary budgets up the organization. The preliminary budgets that senior administrators receive may affect their initial expectations and are either incorporated into the overall athletic department's budget or used as a basis for dialogue with the lower-level coach or administrator who submitted the budget. This feedback loop may continue for several rounds. Once all parties in the process agree on the details, the budget is formally approved by the athletic director or other top administrator and then communicated to the entire athletic department.

Note that although participative budgets are the norm, smaller and less decentralized athletic departments may opt to use a more top-down budgeting process where senior administrators create the budget and simply communicate it to lower-level administrators and coaches. The primary cost of using this more dictatorial method of setting budgets is that it may adversely affect the commitment of lower-level personnel to the budgeted numbers since they did not help create them. This potential cost should not be underemphasized; without buy-in from lower-level personnel, budgets become less useful as a management and decision-making tool.

Using a top-down budgeting process offers several potential benefits. For example, short-term budgets that are imposed by senior administrators are more likely to be consistent with the strategic long-term goals and objectives of the athletic department. When budgets are created using a participative, bottom-up approach, the likelihood is higher that individual program budgets will conflict with the long-term goals and objectives of the athletic department. A second benefit of using a top-down budget is that the budgeting process can be relatively quick because it requires less back-and-forth between senior administrators and lower-level personnel.

Budgets Are Based on Assumptions: Garbage In, Garbage Out

Creating a budget is easy. Creating an accurate budget is not. Creating accurate budgets requires individuals to make valid assumptions about the quantitative impact of multiple future events. This is not a trivial exercise and often involves as much art as science. Typically the more time and effort individuals spend acquiring information and making informed assumptions, the higher the probability is that their budgets will be accurate. The opposite is also true, which is why the term "garbage in, garbage out" is often used to describe the process of making assumptions and creating budgets.

Prudent administrators and coaches rely on several sources of information in settling on the assumptions they ultimately use to prepare their respective budgets—for example, the previous period's budget and actual performance, as well as macroeconomic inputs such as the state of the local economy, the level of competition, and market size. Individuals can access innumerable sources when making assumptions; in fact, the problem they often face is not one of finding sources but rather one of bringing diverse sources together to make a well-justified assumption.

Recent surveys on the budgeting practices of U.S. corporations have found that those responsible for creating budgets tend to rely most heavily on past performance when predicting future performance. For example, a manager might calculate the average growth rate in revenues over the past three periods and then use this rate as the primary source for making an assumption about the growth in revenues next period. This practice is commonly referred to as *incremental budgeting* or *add-on budgeting*, because future budgets are simply past budgets adjusted for an expected incremental increase or decrease next period. Setting budgets in this manner is popular because in most settings, past performance is a reasonable signal of future performance, and starting the budgeting process with data on past performance is much easier than trying to create assumptions from scratch.

It is important to keep in mind that a "good" budget is an accurate budget. An inherent assumption embedded in using the incremental-budgeting approach is that past conditions are often reflective of future conditions. In fact, this may not necessarily be the case, especially in environments where athletic directors and coaches are simultaneously trying to comply with NCAA, conference, and gender equity regulations while dealing with deteriorating economic conditions or other new or fast-changing conditions. Another potential drawback of using an incremental budgeting approach is that individuals tend to be biased toward incorporating incremental increases rather than no changes or incremental decreases. When a program's performance in the previous period was unusual, either exceptionally good or bad, this bias can result in inaccurate budgeted numbers the following period. A final caveat to using an incremental budgeting approach is that it typically assumes that the line items listed in the previous period's budget are valid and do not need to be justified each period going forward. Continually relying on the line items in the previous period's budget can result in outdated and incrementally less accurate budgets going forward.

An alternative approach (albeit one that is quite extreme) to incremental or add-on budgeting is the concept of *zero-based budgeting*. This form of budgeting requires individuals to start fresh each period as if they were creating a budget for the first time. This requires not only thinking about how individual line items will change from period to period, but also whether each line item should be included in the budget. Few business organizations or athletic departments use zero-based budgeting because of the time and resources required for the process. However, new projects, especially ones such as the construction of a stadium that are unlike previous projects, essentially require zero-based budgeting. In addition, periodically requiring administrators and coaches to go through the thought process of creating a zero-based budget can result in more accurate budgets over time.

Keeping Budgets Current: Updating Assumptions

In most athletic departments, the budgeting process is conducted once a year and can take anywhere from a couple of weeks to several months depending on the size of the department and whether the department uses a top-down or participative approach. At the University of Washington, the budgeting process starts in early April and concludes in early June. The timing of the process is typically dictated by an institution's *fiscal year*. A fiscal year is a one-year period used for planning and budgeting purposes, and for state institutions, their fiscal year often coincides with their respective state government's fiscal year. For example, the State of Washington and the University of Washington share the same fiscal year: July 1 to June 30.

NEW DIRECTIONS FOR INSTITUTIONAL RESEARCH • DOI: 10.1002/ir

A lot can happen in only one year. One way to keep administrators and coaches vested throughout the year in the budgeting process is to use *flexible budgets*. A flexible budget incorporates different activity levels for key inputs (such as labor hours or tickets sold). Typically it contains a column for a baseline budget alongside columns for various activity levels. Using flexible budgets allows administrators and coaches to clearly see the financial implications of changes to their key assumption (such as the impact of lower-than-expected ticket sales or student fees). Creating and altering flexible budgets is quite simple using Microsoft Excel. Flexible budgets are commonly used by businesses because they are relatively easy to implement. Even flexible budgets, however, may not accurately capture the impact of operating in rapidly changing environments. A more radical approach, and one that is also much more time-consuming to implement, is the use of *rolling* (or continuous) *budgets*.

Under a rolling-budget system, administrators and coaches within an athletic department prepare budgets for a fixed number of periods. For example, everyone might prepare budgets for each of the four quarters within a year. The four quarters do not have to match up with the athletic department's fiscal year, though having the first rolling budget start at the beginning of the fiscal year simplifies the process. At the end of each period, administrators and coaches update their budgets for all subsequent periods and add on a new period at the end. For the University of Washington, this means that administrators and coaches update their budgets for the next three quarters (October–December, January–March, and April–June) and then add a budget for an additional quarter (July–September). As a result of individuals' continuously updating and adding a period to their budgets, rolling budgets always contain a constant number of periods. These budgets can help administrators and coaches make informed decisions using current information, but only if those responsible for updating and adding on to their budgets actively participate in the process each period. If not, the old adage of "garbage in, garbage out" applies.

Potential Advantages and Disadvantages of Budgeting

Conventional management accounting textbooks, academic literature, and practitioners in business and intercollegiate athletics suggest that when individuals are committed to and actively involved in the budgeting process, its advantages far outweigh its disadvantages. This section first discusses the primary advantages of using budgets and then several potential disadvantages of using budgets.

- *Better goal alignment and resource allocation.* The budgeting process compels administrators and coaches to think about their program's goals and the financial implications of those goals. It also forces them to consider how their goals align with the overall goals of the athletic department. As a result, budgets tend to facilitate the efficient allocation of scarce resources across programs within an athletic department. They also serve the role of an explicit or implicit contract between senior administrators and lower-level personnel with respect to the allocation of resources and performance expectations.

- *Improved communication and coordination.* The budgeting process, particularly one that is participative, facilitates communication within an athletic department. Communicating with those above, below, and at the same level within an individual's departmental hierarchy helps align the individual's goals and objectives with the goals and objectives of others.

- *Increased motivation and performance measurement.* Budgets can be used for incentive purposes to motivate individuals to achieve a desired level of performance. When used in this manner, administrators and coaches who meet or beat their budgeted numbers (by either generating more revenue or incurring lower expenses relative to the budget) can be explicitly rewarded according to their incentive compensation contracts. Using budgets in this manner is quite common in the business world and is becoming more common in intercollegiate athletics. Academic research shows that providing individuals with incentives to achieve challenging but realistically attainable budget targets effectively motivates them to exert effort towards achieving the targets (Merchant and Manzoni, 1989; Tully, 1994).

- *Improved attitude.* Budgets can be used to affect the attitudes and behaviors of individuals. Lower-level administrators and coaches who are actively involved in the budgeting process are more likely to internalize the goals and objectives of the athletic department and work toward achieving them. They are also more likely to feel a sense of accomplishment when budget targets are met or exceeded.

- *Better control.* Budgets are used as a control device to assess whether the athletic department and individual programs are moving toward achieving their goals and objectives. Comparing the difference between actual results and budgeted figures allows administrators and coaches to assess the validity of their original assumptions and, if needed, plan alternate courses of action. When used in this manner, budgets can serve as an early warning sign that original expectations were either unrealistically low or high and that potential corrective actions are needed.

Although most athletic departments use budgets for planning or performance assessment purposes, or both, budgets also have several potential disadvantages:

- *Increased gamesmanship.* Directly linking administrators' or coaches' compensation to budgeted numbers may encourage gamesmanship in the budget-setting process, as well as in activities that managers choose to pursue so that they can meet or beat their respective budgets. For exam-

NEW DIRECTIONS FOR INSTITUTIONAL RESEARCH • DOI: 10.1002/ir

ple, if a coach's compensation depends on the number of games won during a season, the coach may choose to schedule games against weaker opponents to increase the probability of winning more games. It is possible that tension exists between senior administrators and lower-level personnel with respect to what constitutes an acceptable performance threshold. On one hand, senior administrators have an incentive to set high budget targets in an attempt to maximize the effort put forth by lower-level administrators and coaches. On the other hand, the lower-level administrators and coaches whose performance will be measured against the budget have an incentive to prepare a *slack budget*—one that is easier to attain than an honest estimate. By proposing a slack budget, individuals not only reduce the expectations of senior administrators, but also increase the chance that they will meet their targets and be awarded additional compensation. Since senior administrators are often dependent on lower-level administrators and coaches for information about their respective programs, lower-level personnel typically have the ability to influence their budget targets. Thus, it is important to keep in mind that any line item in a budget that is linked to an individual's compensation may be padded with slack in order to maximize the chance that the individual will meet the budget target.

- *Wasteful spending.* Besides these gaming behaviors, budgets can create a "use it or lose it" mentality. This wasteful behavior is particularly prevalent when next period's budget is simply a reflection of last period's actual performance plus an adjustment. When budgets are set in this manner, administrators and coaches have an incentive to use their entire budget or risk receiving less next period. A sign of this type of behavior is excessive spending at the end of a budget period. One potential way to mitigate this behavior is to provide individuals with incentives to maximize sources of revenues and minimize expenses so that their behavior is more closely aligned with the athletic departments' overall goals and objectives.

- *Consumption of time and resources.* Acquiring and analyzing multiple sources of information, as well as creating and updating budgets, takes time and resources. This is especially true when the goals and objectives of senior administrators differ from those of lower-level administrators and coaches. When this is the case, agreeing on a budget may take considerable time and effort.

Conclusion

Being an effective leader in intercollegiate athletics requires an understanding of how to acquire, analyze, and use financial information to make informed decisions. Two important skills that fall under this broad requirement are knowing how to access and use external sources of financial information to make informed decisions and knowing how to prepare and use budgets to make informed decisions. This chapter introduced these skills. Our goal in doing so is to plant a seed that we hope will grow among tomorrow's leaders in intercollegiate athletics.

References

Berkowitz, S. "IMG Jolts Campus Scene to Give Schools a Cash Boost." *USA Today,* Apr. 2, 2009, p. C1.
Merchant, K. A., and Manzoni, J. F. "The Achievability of Budget Targets in Profit Centers: A Field Study." *Accounting Review,* 1989, *64,* 539–558.
National Collegiate Athletic Association. "Current Budgeted Revenues Chart." 2009. Retrieved July 10, 2009, from http://ncaa.org.
Tully, S. "Why Go for Stretch Targets." *Fortune,* 1994, *130*(10), 145–158.

FRANK HODGE is the Herbert O. Whitten Professor of Accounting at the University of Washington's Foster School of Business.

LLOYD TANLU is an assistant professor at the University of Washington's Foster School of Business.

NEW DIRECTIONS FOR INSTITUTIONAL RESEARCH • DOI: 10.1002/ir

2

This chapter presents the history behind the movement to collect data on intercollegiate athletics.

Making Money—or Not—on College Sports

Welch Suggs

One day, stroll around the athletics facilities at a big-time college. Check out the football stadium, where row upon row of stands are topped by massive edifices containing opulent skyboxes, airy press boxes, and banks upon banks of lights for night games. Wander through the weight rooms. Finally, walk down to the athletics department's business office, which is probably on the same corridor as the athletics media relations office, the sports marketing office, and perhaps the department for academic advising, medical consultation, and other areas. If asked politely and if the university is public, the associate athletics director in charge of business affairs will probably provide you with a copy of the department's budget.

Yet no matter how much experience in finance you might have, you will not be able to definitely determine how much this intercollegiate athletics program costs the university whose name it bears. Nor will you be able to make rigorous comparisons between this athletics department and those of its rivals, let alone other big-time programs elsewhere in the country.

Organizations such as the National Collegiate Athletic Association (NCAA) and the Knight Commission, as well as many members of the press, have debated for years whether intercollegiate athletics departments make money. In 2003, an NCAA study noted that 85 of the then 117 institutions in Division I-A, the highest competitive level of intercollegiate athletics, reported a positive cash flow (Fulks, 2004). That study further notes that if one discounts the general-fund subventions, scholarship supplements, and

NEW DIRECTIONS FOR INSTITUTIONAL RESEARCH, no. 144, Winter 2009 © Wiley Periodicals, Inc.
Published online in Wiley InterScience (www.interscience.wiley.com) • DOI: 10.1002/ir.310

student fees transferred from the university to its athletics program, the number drops to 47. Few people believe that many athletics programs are financially stable. Myles Brand (2003), president of the NCAA from 2002–2009, often indicates that only a dozen or fewer athletics departments make money.

Why can't anyone say for certain? Athletics departments have revenues and expenses, and it should not be that hard to ascertain the differences between income and spending. Two answers exist. The first is practical: no trustworthy data set on revenues and expenses currently exist for intercollegiate athletics. This chapter examines the history and shortcomings of the available data collected over the past forty-five years.

The second answer explains the reason for the unavailability of such data. Colleges are nonprofit institutions. This statement is true intuitively and it is true legally, and according to Howard R. Bowen (1980), it is a powerful theory to account for colleges' actions. Colleges do not make decisions to maximize profit, as Bowen points out in *The Costs of Higher Education* (1980). Instead, they make decisions to maximize revenue collections and prestige. As a result, the revenue available for educational purposes determines costs in higher education.

Bowen's analysis covers colleges and universities, particularly in relation to state and private sources of funding. Although he does not consider it, his model offers an intriguing explanation for why most colleges spend much more than they make on intercollegiate athletics and why good data on the finances of college athletics are so difficult to collect.

Athletics departments on college campuses, particularly in Division I, are very interested in the approbation that stems from winning teams. They pursue success on the athletics field with the knowledge, consent, and support of the central university administration because they believe that the goodwill that stems from big games extends beyond the field and into the institution. The scholarly consensus, addressed comprehensively by Robert H. Frank in "Challenging the Myth: A Review of the Links Among College Athletic Success, Student Quality, and Donations" (2004), is that athletics success does not predict higher giving rates, increased numbers of applications, a better cohort of applicants, or any other measure of university success.

The myth dies hard, however, and colleges continue to invest heavily in athletics expecting returns not in the form of profit per se but rather in prestige. For example, Kennesaw State University in metropolitan Atlanta has begun the transition from Division II to Division I as part of a general effort to raise the university's profile to the point that it is considered to be in the same "league" as the University of Georgia or Georgia State University (Kennesaw State University, n.d.).

Athletics administrators raise all the money they can from game day revenue, broadcast royalties, postseason tournament distributions, and sources within the university, such as student fees or tuition waivers. Then they spend all the money they raise, primarily on coaching salaries, team expenses, tuition and expenses for players, administrative expenses, and facilities. Since public institutions receive state funding and limited state oversight, athletics departments receive funds and limited oversight from their institutions. Thus, colleges and their sports programs share the consequences of ever-increasing expenditures (Bowen, 1980).

Because their goal is not to maximize profit, it could be argued that colleges have little need to measure the exact inputs and outputs of particular units or to benchmark those units against peer institutions. Furthermore, athletics departments may not benchmark themselves, citing the need for privacy, differences in organizational framework, or other concerns.

Very little work has been done on the fiscal operations of the roughly seventeen hundred institutions that compete in intercollegiate athletics, in other segments of the NCAA, or in other organizations, with the exception of some basic NCAA financial studies and work on the most selective private institutions in Division III (Bowen and Shulman, 2001). As a result, this chapter confines itself to the study of the "big time"—the colleges in NCAA Division I whose teams compete in front of crowds of thousands every week of the academic year.

I start by reviewing the early history of college sports and continue with an analysis of the most important studies of college sports finance. I then discuss changes in data requirements that came with federal gender equity laws and note more recent quantitative studies of intercollegiate sports finance. Finally, I conclude by offering some potential theoretical positions from which to study the economics and finance of college sports and their relationship to the rest of the university.

Athletics as an Independent University Function

Athletics programs at American colleges evolved out of student groups in the second half of the nineteenth century. Bernstein (2001), Sack and Staurowsky (1998), Sperber (1998), and Thelin (1994) all agree that varsity teams in forms recognizable today were organized parallel to student physical education programs as activities unrelated to the educational program.

Faculty members and journalists were often skeptical about the circuslike atmosphere surrounding such athletics events. As a result, in the early twentieth century, faculty and the press published a number of blistering critiques of the enterprise. The most notable of these came from Howard J. Savage and his colleagues at the Carnegie Foundation for the Advancement of Teaching, who in 1929 published *American College Athletics*, an extensive study of the "history, conduct, and values" of intercollegiate athletics. The grim report found, among other things, that strict organization and commercialization had removed the joy from the game (Savage, Bentley, McGovern, and Smiley, 1929).

Savage and his colleagues maintained that significant revenue enabled colleges to give players great luxuries, special coaching, and publicity agents. The salary of football coaches was seen as a particularly egregious

New Directions for Institutional Research • DOI: 10.1002/ir

expense. A survey of ninety-six coaches found that the highest-paid salary was fourteen thousand dollars per year and the median salary was six thousand dollars. Both salary figures were higher than comparable figures for full professors and roughly equivalent to those of academic deans (Savage, Bentley, McGovern, and Smiley, 1929). In addition, Savage reported that alumni often schemed to pay players under the table for their services.

Mark F. Bernstein (2001) has offered one of the most thorough and intriguing analyses of the early finance of intercollegiate athletics. According to Bernstein, the abuses Savage and his colleagues found in 1929 were nearly forty years old. He further states that the University of Pennsylvania's student-run Athletic Association was $6,600 in debt by 1894 and had to turn to the university's alumni to bail it out. By 1906, the Athletic Association at Penn had an administrative staff that reported to no one and a budget of $141,000. In 1922, already in debt from a trip to the Rose Bowl, the university tore down Franklin Field and built a new fifty-four-thousand-seat stadium in its place. Four years later, the university added an upper deck. Penn financed the expansion and a new basketball arena with a bond issue that raised $4 million (Bernstein, 2001).

Throughout the rest of the twentieth century, intercollegiate athletics grew in size and stature. Today it is a multibillion-dollar industry with more than a thousand colleges participating in NCAA sports. However, data on the operational needs and outcomes of athletics departments have been scarce and difficult to come by throughout most of the past century.

The Modern Scholarship on Intercollegiate Athletics Finance

In 1969, the NCAA commissioned its first in an ongoing series of reports on the finance of intercollegiate athletics, selecting the University of Missouri's accounting department to lead this project. Mitchell H. Raiborn, who left Missouri for Louisiana State University while completing the research, sent questionnaires to the 655 members of the NCAA and received only 277 responses, an overall response rate of 42 percent, making the entire project statistically dubious (Raiborn, 1970). The data covered the 1968–1969 academic year. Writing nearly a decade before the NCAA grouped its members into Divisions I, II, and III, Raiborn came up with his own five-category classification system for institutions, largely along the question of football competitiveness.

Raiborn's data have many limitations. The surveys were entirely voluntary and were forwarded anonymously to the author, meaning he had no way to verify the data or who submitted them. The reports required no internal validation from respondents—that is, financial officers of the institution did not have to certify that the data were accurate. Finally, the form of the survey gave no sense of whether colleges were using comparable accounting definitions. For example, athletics dining halls and residence hall operations were defined by the report as a minor source of revenue for athletics departments. Yet during this era, campuses may have treated such operations in a variety of ways. Some colleges undoubtedly financed training tables and athletics dorms for athletes out of general funds. Some athletics departments may have been able to pay for these services themselves, using revenue generated from ticket sales and revenue. Or fans may have agreed to cover the costs themselves to curry favor with athletes and administrators.

Thus, from the very start, problematic data collection and analyses have obfuscated meaningful attempts to account for the revenues and expenses of intercollegiate athletics departments. Such problems mutated as sources of data changed over time, but they have not been mitigated.

With these caveats in mind, Raiborn's data present some interesting conclusions for what he termed "Class A institutions"—those that participated in football and other sports at the highest level. Revenues as reported increased by more than 100 percent for athletics departments over the course of the 1960s, buoyed largely by increases in ticket sales and game guarantees (in other words, fees paid to visiting teams) for football and basketball teams (Raiborn, 1970). Students provided about 12 percent of departmental revenues in student ticket sales and other assessments. However, Raiborn never discussed whether departments received any kind of direct subsidy from university general funds, even though 20 percent of institutions reported that athletics department deficits were financed by university funds.

The fastest-growing expenses, according to Raiborn's surveys, were scholarships and salaries. However, he noted that programs were expanding, with an average increase of sixty-two athletes per institution (for all respondents, not just Class A members), meaning that expenses might not have been rising on a per capita basis (Raiborn, 1970). Capital expenditures merit only a paragraph in the survey: the valuation of athletics plants grew from $1.8 million in 1960 to $3.5 million in 1969 and were largely financed from non-athletic sources (Raiborn, 1970).

Raiborn's studies were so limited as to be useless as tools for analyzing the finance of intercollegiate athletics, particularly as verification of his findings was impossible. But they set the stage for future research and do provide the earliest version of the basic taxonomy of intercollegiate athletics programs: rich, not so rich, and different gradations of poor.

The Numbers Do Not Tell the Whole Story

The American Council on Education's (ACE) analysis of college sports began with George Hanford's *An Inquiry into the Need for and Feasibility of a National Study of Intercollegiate Athletics* (1974). Hanford, then vice president of the College Entrance Examination Board, pointed out that football produced net revenue at only a few institutions and generated enormous deficits at others. Robert H. Atwell, who later became president of ACE, picked up on Hanford's (1974) and Raiborn's (1970) work through a series of monographs, culminating in the 1980 publication of *The Money Game: Financing Intercollegiate Athletics* (coauthored with Grimes and Lopiano).

Atwell and his coauthors said that while the National Center for Education Statistics had brought some standardization in reporting financial data to higher education, no such efforts had been made in intercollegiate athletics. Interinstitutional comparisons were extraordinarily difficult because of the dearth of standardized data. It could be that athletics directors might have realized profits they did not want to disclose to college administrators or because they did not want to reveal the extent of their dependence on university funds and private gifts.

The authors describe "semiprofessional" departments, which are committed to being nationally competitive in one or more sports and in spending. Debt service for capital improvements made up 10 to 12 percent of operating budgets, and the highest expenses were salaries and wages (25 to 30 percent), scholarships (18 to 20 percent), and recruiting and travel (12 to 15 percent) (Atwell, Grimes, and Lopiano, 1980). On the revenue side, gate receipts provided 50 percent of departmental income, with television and bowl receipts adding 10 to 15 percent. Student fees accounted for 10 percent of program revenue at institutions with football programs and 20 percent at those without football (Atwell, Grimes, and Lopiano,1980).

Atwell, Grimes, and Lopiano asserted that little, if any, institutional support goes into operating budgets for athletics at the universities they designate as semiprofessional. A few institutions supported salaries or scholarships, or both, out of general funds, but at most colleges, institutional support consisted of providing the physical plant and utilities for athletics departments.

This volume was one of the first articulations of some commonly accepted truths about college sports: only a few teams generate profits in excess of expenses, institutions support "semiprofessional" programs by providing facilities and utilities free of charge, and national organizations exercise more control over intercollegiate athletics than colleges themselves do. However, its data set was so small that it did not provide a very comprehensive grasp of how colleges spent money on athletics. That did not change until the 1990s.

Title IX and Reporting Requirements

Bowen (1980) had indicated that colleges make decisions not to maximize profit but to maximize revenues and prestige, thus making the revenue available for educational purposes determine the costs in higher education. This tendency is demonstrated in colleges' expansion of their sports offerings. But such expansions, as well as associated increases in costs, also have occurred because of the need to comply with Title IX of the Education Amendments of 1972, which bans sex discrimination at institutions receiving federal funds (Suggs, 2005). Nearly two decades later, Title IX became the impetus for a new set of data reporting requirements for athletics programs.

In 1994, Congress passed the Equity in Athletics Disclosure Act (EADA), which required colleges to publish summary versions of the data they had been providing to the NCAA for Raiborn's reports, which were published every two years beginning in 1970. Specifically, colleges had to report the number of students on each men's and women's team, the amount of money spent on athletics scholarships for male and female student athletes, the numbers of male and female coaches for men's and women's teams, and the total revenues and expenses (including an itemization that outlines the revenues and expenses from football, men's basketball, women's basketball, all other men's sports combined, and all other women's sports combined) derived from the institution's intercollegiate athletics activities.

The EADA required colleges to begin publishing reports on this information following the 1995–1996 academic year. The NCAA devised a form consisting of a number of worksheets and ten tables and required members to submit them annually. These reports then became the basis of the association's biennial reports on the revenues and expenses of intercollegiate athletics, which Daniel L. Fulks took over from Raiborn in 1995. Fulks's EADA data allowed him to adjust figures to remove institutional support, that is, direct transfer of institutional funds to athletics programs, including student fees (except for student ticket sales). He does not restate average revenues but shows that most Division I-A athletics departments depend heavily on funding from their institutions. Exempting institutional funding, Fulks (2004) finds that intercollegiate athletics can balance the books at fewer than fifty institutions in Division I-A.

Beyond strictly profits and losses, Fulks's (2004) definitions of revenue and expense line items are sufficiently different to prevent direct comparisons with Raiborn's data. On average, ticket sales account for 27 percent of departmental revenue; donations account for 9 percent; institutional support for 10 percent; and postseason revenue from the NCAA, bowl games, and other sources for 14 percent. This reflects the new revenue available to institutions from the NCAA's contracts to broadcast the Division I men's basketball tournament as well as television broadcast deals made by conferences to show football and basketball games (Fulks, 2004). Salaries for both coaches and administrators account for nearly a third of departmental expenses. Scholarships represent 18 percent, while equipment and supplies are now only 4 percent.

Fulks has access to both the worksheets and tables that colleges send to the NCAA, but only the ten tables, which contain summary data, are made public under the EADA. Using newly available database technology, newspapers began collecting data aggressively, with the *Chronicle of Higher Education*, *Kansas City Star*, *New York Times*, *USA Today*, and *Washington Post* publishing reports on college athletics as the data became available. (The reports are available from the U.S. Department of Education at http://ope.ed.gov/athletics.)

NEW DIRECTIONS FOR INSTITUTIONAL RESEARCH • DOI: 10.1002/ir

Researchers, however, should be very careful about using this as a trusted resource. The problems that Atwell, Grimes, and Lopiano (1980) identified are as true of EADA-based data as they were in Raiborn's time. Outside analysts have no way of verifying any of the information contained in the reports submitted by colleges to the NCAA, the U.S. Department of Education, and media outlets. Different institutions have a variety of accounting requirements, rendering comparisons among institutions problematic at best.

Partly for this reason, only recently have economists begun to turn their attention to rigorous analysis of intercollegiate athletics financial data.

Bowen and Shulman in *The Game of Life*

Possibly the most controversial study of intercollegiate athletics in the past decade has been *The Game of Life: College Sports and Educational Values* (2001) by William G. Bowen and James L. Shulman. Bowen and Shulman, who were president and chief financial officer, respectively, of the Andrew W. Mellon Foundation at the time of publication, found that athletes at selective colleges tended to have poorer academic credentials than other students, tended to cluster in the social sciences, and held fewer community leadership positions following graduation.

The findings on academics have been hotly disputed even years after the book was published, but Bowen's (a president emeritus of Princeton and an economist by training) and Shulman's chapter on expenditures and revenues has received virtually no attention. Their findings are necessarily limited, especially regarding big-time college sports, because their analysis covered only twenty-two institutions. These included only eight in Division I-A: Duke University, University of Michigan, Northwestern University, Pennsylvania State University, University of Notre Dame, Stanford University, Tulane University, and Vanderbilt. All were chosen not because of their sports prestige but because of the selectivity of their admissions processes (Bowen and Shulman, 2001).

As earlier analysts have found, Bowen and Shulman note the high cost of athletics scholarships and employee salaries, particularly those of coaches. However, they make an attempt to separate teams' operating costs from infrastructure costs (administration, marketing, physical plant, and so forth). The top Division I-A colleges in their sample—Michigan, Notre Dame, Penn State, and Stanford—spent $16 million annually on infrastructure costs on average, or 44 percent on average, of their intercollegiate athletics budgets (Bowen and Shulman, 2001).

The authors discussed the weaknesses of EADA data and then opted instead for a case study approach, looking at Michigan and Duke, among other institutions. In 1997–1998, Michigan earned $30 million and Duke $10 million in athletics-related revenue. Most of these funds came from gate receipts, sponsorship in licensing fees, fundraising, television, and post-

NEW DIRECTIONS FOR INSTITUTIONAL RESEARCH • DOI: 10.1002/ir

season revenue, thanks to both institutions' avid fan bases and winning teams in football (Michigan) and basketball (Duke).

The question of overhead and capital costs is the most important and most elusive part of the equation, the authors argue. A portion of the president's salary, the admission's office's time, and similar fractions of other campus operations should be figured in any sort of overall reckoning of the cost of intercollegiate athletics on a campus, they said. As for capital costs, the athletics physical plant at Princeton has been valued at $200 million; they reckon that the comparable figure at Duke or Northwestern would be double that and assume that "the University of Michigan, with its huge athletic complex, lives in a capital cost stratosphere of its own" (Bowen and Shulman, 2001, p. 250). This was the first iteration of the Mellon study.

Is There an Arms Race in College Sports?

Following the publication of *The Game of Life*, the Mellon Foundation and the NCAA jointly funded two studies of intercollegiate athletics by Sebago Associates, a firm consisting of Robert E. Litan, Jonathan N. Orszag, and Peter R. Orszag (2003; Orszag and Orszag, 2005). The reports applied much more sophisticated economic techniques to EADA reports and other sources of data than had been done before, finding that athletics expenditures in Division I-A are a relatively small share of overall academic spending. At the same time, the report showed that Division I-A football and basketball markets exhibit increasing levels of inequality, as well as some degree of mobility in expenditure, revenue, and winning percentages—colleges move somewhat freely among quartiles in these areas over time.

A second report, issued in 2005, suggested that there might be a subtle arms race in football capital spending in Division I-A, given that the expansion of a stadium within a conference appears to make it more likely that other schools within the conference will expand the capacity of their stadiums (Orszag and Orszag, 2005).

While the study by Orszag and Orszag (2005) applied more of an econometric approach, as opposed to the accounting approach favored by Raiborn, Fulks, and Bowen and Shulman, their data limitations made it impossible to conclude whether spending on college sports was a drain on institutional finances or whether universities were engaged in an "arms race" to improve facilities. EADA data suggest that athletics department operating budgets are indeed a small portion of university operating funds, but as Bowen and Shulman (2001) point out, such analyses neglect both the capital costs of sports programs and the real costs that should be attributed to athletics programs, such as the time of administrators outside athletics departments. Even Orszag and Orszag's attempts to discuss the "arms race" fell short because it included only capacity changes at college stadiums, not the multimillion-dollar expansions of academic facilities, training complexes, and elaborate coaches' offices emerging across the country. Jonathan Orszag has added additional studies to the NCAA's libraries but has not been able to get past this challenge.

Other Discussions

Little progress has been made in the understanding of intercollegiate athletics finance. Ticket receipts, television royalties, postseason distributions, game guarantees, and institutional transfers remain the main source of income for intercollegiate athletics, although the last is highly difficult to assess without overall university budgets to study. An athletics department's key challenge is to ascertain its best chances of maximizing each source of revenue, which will vary based on a number of factors, including teams' competitive records, conference affiliations, and the market power of athletics departments. A research team led by John V. Lombardi, chancellor of the University of Massachusetts at Amherst, noted that this has significant ramifications for the opportunity cost generated by athletics programs (Lombardi and others, 2003). An institution with an annual budget of $700 million that must subsidize an athletics program with $8 million in general fund subventions has an opportunity cost equal to 1.14 percent of its budget.

A new contribution to the literature is an edited volume by John Fizel and Rodney Fort: *The Economics of College Sports* (2004). Its authors examine the topic from a variety of angles, including perspectives on the NCAA and the political market it has created, marginal revenue production for athletes, and competitive balance within college sports. On the question of institution-level finance, Brian Goff (2004) notes that departments value athletics scholarships at their "list price" rather than the actual marginal cost of housing and educating each athlete, and athletically produced revenues, notably merchandise sales, are often credited to general funds or nonathletics units. Goff goes on to suggest that making such adjustments indicates that most institutions actually do make money: of 109 Division I-A institutions, he estimates that the median profit on athletics operations among big-time institutions is $3.9 million, and 26 percent of universities turn a profit of $7.1 million or more.

Conclusions and Recommendations for Further Research

It is a common truism that the economic landscape of college athletics has been completely redrawn in the past few decades. The rivers of revenue have shifted somewhat in their courses, with television and postseason revenue, along with ticket revenue, coming to dominate the decisions made by directors of major athletics programs. However, the basic structure and motivations of athletics departments have not changed in more than a century. It can be argued that, similar to what Bowen proffered with respect to the motivations for costs escalations in higher education, even athletics departments spend money not to make profits but to put the best teams on the field in a way of reflecting greater glory on their own institutions.

Even after plugging away for three decades, economists still have no way of saying how much sports truly cost their institutions, much less what their opportunity costs might be. There is a clear need for better data, which may possibly come from a new reporting system implemented by the NCAA and the National Association of College and University Business Officers (NACUBO) in 2008. Greater uniformity in accounting procedures for intercollegiate athletics revenues and expenses could also create a useful data set for researchers to provide more accurate conclusions about intercollegiate athletics.

Moreover, what is needed is a better application of the principles of economics and finance in higher education. Bowen's revenue theory of cost applies directly to the behavior of athletics departments, which spend money on capital and operational strategies to win games and recruit better athletes. This is a form of prestige maximization rather similar to the one practiced by colleges and universities, whose faculties and administrators would like to attract research grants and better students.

One potential theory to organize future research is resource dependency theory. The basic notion, as laid out by Pfeffer and Salancik (1978), is that an organization's vulnerability to external influence is partly determined by the extent of its dependency on resources provided by outside entities. There are two measures of dependence: the magnitude of the exchange and the criticality of the resource. The overriding long-term organizational goal is autonomy or independence; removing dependence on resource providers ensures continuing stability and equilibrium.

The actions of organizations, and particularly universities, can be understood only by reference to external resource providers. As universities look outward to students, donors, corporations, governments, and other grant makers for funds, this point takes on enormous importance.

The same trend has come about in athletics, in which departmental personnel have come to rely on donors and broadcasting corporations for operating funds. Such organizations thus have some control over departmental operations, most notably in the scheduling of basketball and football games. When ESPN or other broadcast entities demand that games be played on weeknights or late at night without regard for student schedules, observers worry about the influence of commercial entities on college life.

"Nearly a third of our conference revenue comes from broadcast royalties, and nobody is immune to the pressures of the marketplace," said Michael F. Adams, president of the University of Georgia, in a story in the NCAA News (Johnson, 2005). "As you know, schedules in baseball, basketball and softball are even more disruptive not only to campus life, but also to the academic life of the student-athletes involved."

NEW DIRECTIONS FOR INSTITUTIONAL RESEARCH • DOI: 10.1002/ir

In the view of some observers, including Bok (2003) and Slaughter and Rhoades (2004), athletics represents the leading edge of the growing controversy over commercial intrusions on college campuses. Armed with what we hope will be trustworthy new data, scholars will have the opportunity to assess the athletics enterprise for its role and influence on campus life and present new policies to help university officials deal with a seemingly interminable problem.

References

Atwell, R. H., Grimes, B. and Lopiano, D. *The Money Game: Financing Intercollegiate Athletics.* Washington, D.C.: American Council on Education, 1980.

Bernstein, M. F. *Football: The Ivy League Origins of an American Obsession.* Philadelphia: University of Pennsylvania Press, 2001.

Bok, D. C. *Universities in the Marketplace: The Commercialization of Higher Education.* Princeton, N.J.: Princeton University Press, 2003.

Bowen, H. R. *The Costs of Higher Education.* San Francisco: Jossey-Bass, 1980.

Bowen, W. G., and Shulman, J. L. *The Game of Life: College Sports and Educational Values.* Princeton, N.J.: Princeton University Press, 2001.

Brand, M. "A Crossroads in College Sports." Speech to the American Association of University Professors, Indianapolis, Oct., 2003. Retrieved Dec. 8, 2005, from http://www.math.umd.edu/~jmc/COIA/AAUPconference.htm#mb.

Fizel, J., and Fort, R. (eds.). *The Economics of College Sports.* Westport, Conn.: Praeger, 2004.

Frank, R. *Challenging the Myth: A Review of the Links Among College Athletic Success, Student Quality, and Donations.* Miami: Knight Foundation Commission on Intercollegiate Athletics, May 2004. Retrieved Oct. 15, 2009, from http://www.knightcommission.org/index.php?option=com_content&view=article&id=73:challenging-the-myth-a-review-of-the-links-among-college-athletic-success-student-quality-and-donations&catid=8:fiscal-integrity.

Fulks, D. L. *Revenues and Expenses of Intercollegiate Athletics.* Indianapolis: National Collegiate Athletic Association, 2004.

Goff, B. L. *Effects of University Athletics on the University: A Review and Extension of Empirical Assessment.* In J. Fizel and R. Fort (eds.), *The Economics of College Sports.* Westport, Conn.: Praeger, 2004.

Hanford, G. H. *An Inquiry into the Need for and Feasibility of a National Study of Intercollegiate Athletics.* Washington, D.C.: American Council on Education, 1974.

Johnson, G. *Calendar Creep: Once Reserved Solely for Saturday, College Football Has Been Spreading Its Weekday Wings.* Indianapolis: National Collegiate Athletic Association, Nov. 21, 2005. Retrieved Oct. 15, 2009, from http://www.ncaa.org/wps/ncaa?key=/ncaa/ncaa/ncaa+news/ncaa+news+online/2005/division+i/calendar+creep+-+11-21-05+ncaa+news.

Kennesaw State University. "Kennesaw State Athletics—Athletics History." n.d. Retrieved Dec. 8, 2005, from http://ksuowls.kennesaw.edu/division1move.asp.

Litan, R. E., Orszag, J. N., and Orszag, P. R. *The Empirical Effects of Collegiate Athletics: An Interim Report.* Indianapolis: National Collegiate Athletic Association, 2003.

Lombardi, J. V., and others. *The Top American Research Universities 2003.* Gainesville, Fla.: The Center, 2003. Retrieved Nov. 5, 2009, from http://mup.asu.edu/.

Orszag, J. N., and Orszag, P. R. *The Empirical Effects of Collegiate Athletics: An Update.* Indianapolis: National Collegiate Athletic Association, 2005.

Pfeffer, J., and Salancik, G. R. *The External Control of Organizations.* New York: Harper-Collins, 1978.

Raiborn, M. *Financial Analysis of Intercollegiate Athletics*. Mission, Kan.: National Collegiate Athletic Association, 1970.

Sack, A. F., and Staurowsky, E. J. *College Athletes for Hire: The Evolution and Legacy of the NCAA's Amateur Myth*. Westport, Conn.: Praeger, 1998.

Savage, H. J., Bentley, H.W., McGovern, J.T., and Smiley, D.F. *American College Athletics*. New York: Carnegie Foundation for the Advancement of Teaching, 1929.

Slaughter, S., and Rhoades, G. *Academic Capitalism and the New Economy: Markets, State, and Higher Education*. Baltimore: Johns Hopkins University Press, 2004.

Sperber, M. A. *Onward to Victory: The Crises That Shaped College Sports*. New York: Holt, 1998.

Suggs, W. *A Place on the Team: The Triumph and Tragedy of Title IX*. Princeton, N.J.: Princeton University Press, 2005.

Thelin, J. R. *Games Colleges Play: Scandal and Reform in Intercollegiate Athletics*. Baltimore: Johns Hopkins University Press, 1994.

WELCH SUGGS serves as assistant to the president at the University of Georgia and earned his doctorate from the university's Institute of Higher Education in 2009.

NEW DIRECTIONS FOR INSTITUTIONAL RESEARCH • DOI: 10.1002/ir

3

This chapter discusses data sources available for studying the experience of student athletes on college campuses and highlights the need for national-level data to address complex questions concerning this population.

The Student Athlete Experience

Joy Gaston Gayles

Prior to the 1980s, the literature on the experiences of collegiate student athletes was rather scarce. Since that time the National Collegiate Athletic Association (NCAA) has passed several eligibility rules to address concerns about the academic performance and the overall experience of student athletes on college campuses. As such, the literature related to the impact of participation in college sports on student learning and personal development over the past two decades has grown substantially. Although there is still much to learn about the experiences of student athletes in college, we know much more about factors that bear on student learning and personal development for this population than we did twenty years ago. Of particular interest today is the extent to which student athletes benefit from their college experience in ways similar to their nonathlete peers. As future research is conducted on student athletes' college experiences, it is imperative to understand the data sources available to answer key questions for the purpose of developing policy and practice.

Today's Student Athletes

Student athletes on most college campuses today represent a special population of students with unique challenges and needs different from their nonathlete peers. Student athletes on average spend over twenty hours per week in practice or play, sustain bodily injury and fatigue, and miss a fair number of classes when their sport is in season (Watt and Moore, 2001; Wolverton, 2008). These students are also expected to perform well in the

NEW DIRECTIONS FOR INSTITUTIONAL RESEARCH, no. 144, Winter 2009 © Wiley Periodicals, Inc.
Published online in Wiley InterScience (www.interscience.wiley.com) • DOI: 10.1002/ir.311

classroom and earn grades strong enough to maintain their eligibility for playing college sports.

Such academic and athletic demands, particularly for freshman student athletes, can be difficult to balance. Most athletics programs at the Division I level, where the time constraints are most demanding, have high-quality support service programs in place to assist student athletes with managing academic and athletics tasks. These support programs offer a plethora of services and programs designed to enhance the overall experience of student athletes. Despite the extensive programs and services provided by academic support programs, institutional faculty, administrators, and other critics continue to speculate about the engagement of student athletes in the overall college experience and the extent to which they benefit from their overall college experience relative to their peers.

Some of the harshest criticism suggests that athletics programs create a separate culture in which student athletes experience lower levels of academic performance, graduate at lower rates, cluster in certain majors, and are socially segregated from the general student population (Bowen and Levin, 2003; Shulman and Bowen, 2001). Despite efforts by the NCAA to restrict the numbers of student athletes who live together on campus and enforce standards to promote academic success and retention, suspicion about the role of intercollegiate athletics on the college campus continues to exist.

The Student Athlete Experience

The seven principles of good practice in undergraduate education (Chickering and Gamson, 1987) have been widely cited in the literature on how the college experience affects student learning and personal development. Chickering and Gamson developed these principles in response to the growing concern about the quality of undergraduate education. These seven principles—interaction between faculty and students, cooperative learning among students, active learning, prompt feedback, time on task, communication of high expectations, and respect for diverse ways of learning—have been identified and supported in the literature as having a positive impact on important learning outcomes of undergraduate education for all types of students (Chickering and Gamson, 1987; Kuh, 2001). In addition, Astin's theory of involvement (1999) is closely related to the seven principles of good practice because at its core, the theory suggests that when students are involved in meaningful ways in their undergraduate experience, they learn. Thus, the amount of psychological and physical energy students invest in tasks related to the academic experience, such as interacting with faculty and peers, participating in student groups and organizations, and completing academic assignments, is positively related to their overall learning experience and personal development. We know a great deal from the empirical literature about the impact of these practices for students in the general population. However, less is known about the extent to which student athletes engage in such practices and the impact of these kinds of activities on their learning and development.

A few studies in the literature address concerns about the lack of student athletes' engagement in the undergraduate experience and the creation of a separate athlete subculture on campus that is not in line with the academic mission of higher education institutions. However, the weight of the limited evidence to date suggests that student athletes are involved in their undergraduate experience in ways similar to their undergraduate peers (Richards and Aries, 1999; Stone and Strange, 1989; Umbach, Palmer, Kuh, and Hannah, 2006).

In addition to understanding student athletes' engagement on college campuses, another key area of interest in the literature focuses on how participation in athletics influences student learning and personal development. Student learning and personal development are desired outcomes of undergraduate education and have several subcomponents. Particular to student athletes, these subcomponents consist of academic performance, cognitive development, attitudes and values, and psychosocial development (related to career maturity). In studying the effect of athletics on student learning and development, scholars have relied on various data sources to answer key questions about how students grow and what they learn in college.

Several studies have focused on the career maturity of athletes relative to their nonathlete peers, and the evidence in general suggests that athletes tend to differ from their nonathlete peers in their levels of career maturity and psychosocial development (Kennedy and Dimick, 1987; Smallman and Sowa, 1996; Sowa and Gressard, 1983). Furthermore, the bulk of the evidence indicates some key differences between athletes and their peers along one psychosocial dimension: developing purpose. What we know less about is how athletes compare to their peers on other dimensions of psychosocial development, such as developing competence and establishing mature relationships and identity formation, as well as the net impact of participation in college sports on psychosocial outcomes. Related to the impact of participation in intercollegiate athletics on cognitive development, the evidence suggests that participation in college sports may have a negative impact on cognitive development. For example, McBride and Reed (1998) examined differences between athletes and nonathletes' critical thinking skills and found that athletes had lower critical thinking scores, particularly related to open-mindedness, inquisitiveness, and maturity.

Moving beyond understanding differences between athletes and their peers to assessing what factors are important to cognitive development, Pascarella, Bohr, Nora, and Terenzini (1995) examined the effects of participation in college sports on reading comprehension, mathematics, and critical thinking skills in the first year. After controlling for background characteristics and other confounding variables, the authors found that male athletes in football and basketball scored lower in reading comprehension and mathematics compared to nonathletes and athletes in other sports. Furthermore, there were no significant differences between male athletes in sports other than football and men's basketball compared to nonathletes. However, the effects of participation were general, rather than varying in magnitude, for students at different levels on the control variables. Female athletes scored lower than female nonathletes on reading comprehension. Moreover, the effect was conditional on precollege reading comprehension, indicating that female athletes with lower precollege reading comprehension experienced the highest disadvantage in reading comprehension by the end of the first year.

In a follow-up study, Pascarella and others (1999) examined the impact of participation in college sports on cognitive development in the second and third years of college. A major finding was that the conditional effect of precollege reading comprehension for female athletes was not present in this study, which indicates that female athletes do not experience long-term disadvantages in reading comprehension as a result of participating in college sports. Another critical finding was that male athletes in revenue sports may not be experiencing cognitive benefits (as indicated by lower scores in critical thinking) to the extent of other males in college. Further study is needed to understand why intercollegiate athletics has such a negative effect on cognitive outcomes.

The evidence concerning the impact of participation in college sports on cultural attitudes and values is somewhat mixed. The evidence from examining intercollegiate athletics holistically suggests that intercollegiate athletics has a positive impact on the development of cultural values (Whitt and others, 2001; Wolf-Wendel, Toma, and Morphew, 2001). Nevertheless, when certain populations of student athletes are studied, the evidence suggests otherwise. For example, Wolniak, Pierson, and Pascarella (2001) examined the impact of intercollegiate athletics on attitudes and values for male athletes and found that participating in male nonrevenue sports had a negative impact on openness to diversity and challenge. Furthermore, participation in nonrevenue sports, in addition to participation in Greek life, exacerbated the negative impact on openness to diversity compared to participating in nonrevenue sports alone.

Data Sources for Studying Student Athletes' Learning and Personal Development

This brief survey of the literature on student athletes and their experiences reveals that the majority of studies conducted on student athletes use self-collected data from single institutions. In order for colleges and universities to make sound decisions concerning the welfare of college athletes, longitudinal data sources are needed. There are a few such data sources available for shared use.

National Collegiate Athletic Association. The NCAA has a research and education office that provides educational and leadership opportunities for student athletes. In addition, the office collects data on the academic performance and educational experiences of student athletes on college campuses across the country. The research and education Web site publishes information on the academic progress rate (APR) by school, as well as press releases summarizing the APR and graduation rate data for its member institutions. The Web site also provides summary APR data that, with the APR data by school, can be used for secondary analysis.

Graduation rates published by the NCAA have consistently shown that student athletes complete degrees at higher rates compared to students in the general student population. However, when the data are disaggregated by sport, gender, and race, the numbers tell a different story. Several conclusions can be drawn from the evidence to date. First, male athletes tend to enter college and perform at lower levels compared to their peers. Second, athletes who enter college with lower levels of academic achievement tend to have lower first-year grades in college. Third, participation in intercollegiate athletics has been found to increase motivation to complete a college degree.

One of the first surveys commissioned by the President's Commission of the NCAA was conducted in the 1980s. The Association for Institutional Research (AIR) designed the survey to collect data on the role of intercollegiate athletics in higher education from a national representative sample of student athletes and nonathletes at forty-two Division I institutions. A series of reports describe the experience of student athletes on college campuses. In addition, researchers have used these data to study the experiences of African American and female athletes and career expectations for African American male athletes (Sellers and Kuperminc, 1997; Sellers, Kuperminc, and Damas, 1997).

In the mid-1990s, the NCAA administered the Basic Academic Skills Survey (BASS) to a sample of Division I institutions. The BASS consists of three parts: Progress in College (PIC), Social and Group Experiences (SAGE), and Mini-battery of Achievement (MBA). The PIC survey measured student athletes' academic and social experiences, personal goals, and attitudes. The SAGE survey measured high school and college experiences. The MBA survey measured cognitive skills such as reading, writing, mathematics, and factual knowledge. Researchers recently used these data to study the impact of engagement and sport participation on college outcomes. To address this issue, the authors conducted a secondary analysis of the PIC and SAGE components of the BASS (Gayles and Hu, 2009). They found that engaging in educational activities had a positive influence on cognitive and affective outcomes. Moreover, the effect of engaging in educational activities had differential effects across levels of sport.

The NCAA education and research office currently publishes reports on its Web site about the student athlete population in terms of gender, race/ethnicity, injuries, substance use, and sports wagering. This information provides descriptive data about student athletes on today's college campuses that can be used for trend analyses concerning how student athletes change over time.

The education and research office is responsible for collecting survey data on the experiences of student athletes. During the early 2000s, the NCAA research office funded research projects that focused on the student athlete collegiate experience. In 2004, researchers at the University of Nebraska received funding and administrative support from the NCAA to study college athletes' experiences at eighteen Division I-A schools across the country (Potuto and O'Hanlon, 2006). Overall, student athletes in the study reported positive experiences with participating in college sports. However, the findings were mixed regarding the extent to which participants viewed themselves as athletes more than students and whether professors discriminated against or showed favoritism toward student athletes. In addition, the NCAA education and research office periodically conducts surveys that are available for shared use by interested researchers.

National Survey of Student Engagement. The National Survey of Student Engagement (NSSE) is administered by the Indiana University Center for Postsecondary Research and the Indiana University Center for Survey Research. Since 2000, Indiana University has administered NSSE on an annual basis to various four-year colleges and universities across the country. To date over twelve hundred colleges and universities have participated in this project.

Scholars at Indiana University designed NSSE to assess undergraduate educational experiences, particularly concerning how students spend their time and what they gain from the college experience. Data from the NSSE have been used to formulate five benchmarks that represent good practices in education similar to the seven principles of good practice developed by Chickering and Gamson (1987): level of academic challenge, active and collaborative learning, student-faculty interaction, enriching educational experiences, and supportive campus environments (Kuh, 2001).

Identifying good educational practices for student athletes and potential conditional effects of those practices warrants further research in the literature on the experiences of student athletes. NSSE could serve as a potential data source to address such questions. An item on the demographic portion of the survey asks students if they participate in varsity sports at the institution. When this question was first asked, it did not differentiate student athletes by sport; however, the 2009 administration of the survey asks student athletes to identity the sport(s) in which they participate.

Only one study to date has used NSSE data to examine the engagement practices and educational gains of student athletes compared to their non-athlete peers. Umbach, Palmer, Kuh, and Hannah (2006) used the spring 2003 administration of NSSE data, which contains a sample of

57,308 freshmen students across 395 four-year colleges and universities of varying institutional types. The spring 2003 administration included an item to assess whether students participated in varsity sports but did not assess the type of sport. Therefore, the researchers were not able to disaggregate the data by sport. Overall the authors found that student athletes were as engaged in educational activities compared to their nonathlete peers. In fact, the authors found that student athletes were more satisfied with the college experience and perceived their campus environment to be more supportive. There were a few interesting findings related to the impact of being a student athlete at different institutional types, as defined by the divisions of the NCAA. Student athletes at the Division III level were more engaged compared to student athletes at Division I and II institutions.

Higher Education Research Institute. The Cooperative Institutional Research Program, in conjunction with Higher Education Research Institute (HERI) at the University of California, Los Angeles, administers several surveys, some of which can be used to study attitudes, values, and experiences of college students. The College Students' Beliefs and Values (CSBV) survey is administered by the Spirituality in Higher Education Project at UCLA and can be used in conjunction with CIRP data (also collected by HERI) to study student athletes. The CSBV is a multiyear survey designed to assess trends and patterns related to college students' spirituality and religiousness, as well as the impact of college on spiritual and faith development. The survey began in 2003 with administering the survey to thirty-seven hundred juniors across a representative sample of four-year colleges and universities. The institute collected these data in conjunction with the institutions that participated in the CIRP freshman survey three years prior to 2003.

The religious and spiritual values of college athletes represent an understudied topic that deserves attention in the literature. The CSBV is a potential data source to study the religious and spiritual experiences and values of college athletes because it includes an item on whether the student is a varsity athlete and a follow-up question to determine the level of sport.

Gayles and Bryant (2009) used the CSBV to examine the impact of participation in varsity sports on civic engagement. In particular, they studied the impact of athletic participation on social activism, defined as an individual's general concern for and commitment to making the world a better place. The researchers also examined the extent to which the factors that influence social activism were conditional on the level of sport in which the student athlete participated. The findings from this study suggest that athletes did not differ from their nonathlete peers in their commitment to social activism. Furthermore, athletic participation alone did not influence student athletes' level of social activism. Finally, the factors that affected students' levels of social activism were generally uniform across level of sport.

Conclusion

This chapter focused on what we know about today's student athletes and their experiences on college campuses, as well as how we know. Using large-scale data provides the best opportunity to study the experiences of student athletes and provides the freedom to generalize to the larger student athlete population. Single-institutional and other small-scale studies have the potential to provide valuable information at the institutional level; however, large-scale data sources with representative samples should be relied on most heavily for decision-making purposes at the national level. Not only do such data sources allow researchers to generalize to larger populations, but they also allow researchers to conduct more sophisticated statistical analyses and to address more complex problems concerning the experiences of student athletes.

References

Astin, A. W. "Student Involvement: A Developmental Theory for Higher Education." *Journal of College Student Development*, 1999, 40, 518–529.

Bowen, W. G., and Levin, S. A. *Reclaiming the Game: College Sports Educational Values.* Princeton, N.J.: Princeton University Press, 2003.

Chickering, A. W., and Gamson, Z. F. "Seven Principles for Good Practice in Undergraduate Education." *AAHE Bulletin*, 1987, 39(7), 3–7.

Gayles, J. G., and Bryant, A. N. "The Impact of Athletic Participation on College Students' Commitment to Social Activism." Paper presented at the Annual Meeting of the American Educational Research Association, San Diego, Calif., Apr. 2009.

Gayles, J. G., and Hu, S. "The Influence of Student Engagement and Sport Participation on College Outcomes Among Division I Student Athletes." *Journal of Higher Education*, 2009, 80(3), 315–333.

Kennedy, S. R., and Dimick, K. M. "Career Maturity and Professional Sports Expectations of College Football and Basketball Players." *Journal of College Student Personnel*, 1987, 28(4), 293–297.

Kuh, G. D. "Assessing What Really Matters to Student Learning: Inside the National Survey of Student Engagement." *Change*, 2001, 33(3), 10–17, 66.

McBride, R. E., and Reed, J. "Thinking and College Athletes: Are They Predisposed to Critical Thinking?" *College Student Journal*, 1998, 32, 443–450.

Pascarella, E. T., and others. "Cognitive Impacts of Intercollegiate Athletic Participation: Some Further Evidence." *Journal of Higher Education*, 1999, 70(1), 1–26.

Pascarella, E. T., Bohr, L., Nora, A., and Terenzini, P. T. "Intercollegiate Athletic Participation and Freshmen-Year Cognitive Outcomes." *Journal of Higher Education*, 1995, 66(4), 369–387.

Potuto, J. R., and O'Hanlon, J. "National Study of Student Athletes Regarding Their Experiences as College Students." Indianapolis: National Collegiate Athletic Association, 2006.

Richards, S., and Aries, E. "The Division III Student-Athlete: Academic Performance, Campus Involvement, and Growth." *Journal of College Student Development*, 1999, 40(3), 211–218.

Sellers, R., and Kuperminc, G. P. "Goal Discrepancy in African American Male Student-Athletes' Unrealistic Expectations for Careers in Professional Sports." *Journal of Black Psychology*, 1997, 23(1), 6–23.

Sellers, R. M., Kuperminc, G. P., and Damas, A. "The College Life Experiences of African American Women Athletes." *American Journal of Community Psychology*, 1997, 25(5), 699–720.

Shulman, J. L., and Bowen, W. G. *The Game of Life: College Sports and Educational Values.* Princeton, N.J.: Princeton University Press, 2001.

Smallman, E., and Sowa, C. J. "Career Maturity Levels of Male Intercollegiate Varsity Athletes." *Career Development Quarterly*, 1996, 44, 270–277.

Sowa, C. J., and Gressard, C. F. "Athletic Participation: Its Relationship to Student Development." *Journal of College Student Personnel*, 1983, 24, 236–239.

Stone, J., and Strange, C. "Quality of Student Experiences of Freshmen Intercollegiate Athletes." *Journal of College Student Development*, 1989, 30, 148–154.

Umbach, P. D., Palmer, M. M., Kuh, G. D., and Hannah, S. J. "Intercollegiate Athletes and Effective Educational Practices: Winning Combination or Losing Effort?" *Research in Higher Education*, 2006, 47(6), 709–733.

Watt, S. K., and Moore, J. L. "Who Are Student Athletes?" In S. Watt & J. Moore (eds.), *Student Services for Athletes: New Directions for Student Services*, no. 93. San Francisco: Jossey-Bass, 2001.

Whitt, E. J., and others. "Influences on Students' Openness to Diversity and Challenge in the Second and Third Years of College." *Journal of Higher Education*, 2001, 72(2), 172–204.

Wolf-Wendel, L. E., Toma, D., and Morphew, C. C. "There's No 'I' in 'Team': Lessons from Athletics on Community Building." *Review of Higher Education*, 2001, 24(4), 369–396.

Wolniak, G. C., Pierson, C. T., and Pascarella, E. T. "Effects of Intercollegiate Athletics Participation on Male Orientations Toward Learning." *Journal of College Student Development*, 2001, 42(6), 604–624.

Wolverton, B. "Athletes' Hours Renew Debate over College Sports." *Chronicle of Higher Education*, Jan. 25, 2008. Retrieved June 5, 2008, from http://chronicle.com.

JOY GASTON GAYLES *is associate professor in the Department of Leadership, Policy, Adult, and Higher Education at North Carolina State University.*

NEW DIRECTIONS FOR INSTITUTIONAL RESEARCH • DOI: 10.1002/ir

4

*Data on sport participation rates and gender equity can
be useful to colleges and universities for decision making
and ensuring compliance.*

Gender Equity, Sport Sponsorship, and Participation

Athena Yiamouyiannis

As the pressure to win in select collegiate sports escalates, financial pressures mount, and the need to comply with Title IX regulations and gender equity policies continues, athletics administrators are faced with having to make difficult decisions regarding their sport programs. To assist in the decision-making process regarding sport programs, this chapter focuses on data sources related to gender equity, sport sponsorship, and participation. It centers on how these data can be used for purposes of program evaluation within athletics departments, as well as their use in the policy development and decision-making process.

Title IX, Gender Equity, and Sport Sponsorship Legislation

A review of the federal requirements of Title IX, the National Collegiate Athletic Association's (NCAA) sport sponsorship requirements, and a familiarity with available NCAA and Equity in Athletics Disclosure Act (EADA) data are not only useful when making decisions on sport sponsorship and participation opportunities; they can help athletics administrators avoid some of the unintended consequences (including lawsuits, hidden costs, and so on) that have resulted when insufficient information is considered. This section includes a brief overview of Title IX's athletics regulations, the NCAA's

NEW DIRECTIONS FOR INSTITUTIONAL RESEARCH, no. 144, Winter 2009 © Wiley Periodicals, Inc.
Published online in Wiley InterScience (www.interscience.wiley.com) • DOI: 10.1002/ir.312

philosophy statement on gender equity, information on NCAA sport sponsorship requirements, and NCAA financial aid restrictions.

Title IX's Athletics Regulations. Title IX is a federal law adopted in 1972 that requires gender-equitable access to colleges and universities. Title IX's athletics policies (1979) stipulate that colleges receiving federal funds must provide men and women students with equitable sport participation opportunities, equitable scholarships, and equitable treatment in the provision of benefits and services, such as facilities, equipment and supplies, coaching, publicity, and travel (Title IX and Intercollegiate Athletics: A Policy Interpretation, 1979).

To determine whether a college is providing equitable sport participation opportunities, a three-pronged test is used. A college must meet only one of the three prongs to be considered compliant with Title IX's equitable sport participation opportunity provision. To comply with the first prong (proportionality), the percentage of male and female student athletes should reflect the student body. For example, if the student body is 52 percent women and 48 percent men, the percentage of athletes should be approximately 52 percent women and 48 percent men. To comply with the second prong, the college must have a history and continuing practice of program expansion for the underrepresented gender, such as adding sports for women and expanding the squad size of existing women's sport teams. To comply with the third prong, a college must accommodate the interests and abilities of the underrepresented gender. For example, in cases where women are the underrepresented gender, if there are enough women with sufficient skills and interest to add and sustain a given sport as a varsity team and there is competition in the school's normal competitive region, a school would need to add the sport to comply with the third prong. Regarding the first prong, in 1996 the Office for Civil Rights (OCR) issued a clarification document titled "Clarification of Intercollegiate Athletics Policy Guidance: The Three-Part Test" (U.S. Department of Education, 1996). For prong 1, participation must be "substantially proportionate" to undergraduate enrollment and allows for natural variances from year to year, such as slight enrollment fluctuations. However, if a sport team can be added for the underrepresented gender, then prong 1 is probably not being met. For example, an institution with 600 athletes that is 47 percent female and has a 52 percent female enrollment represents a 62-person gap, which is plenty enough to field a viable team. For prong 2, OCR reviews the history of previously developing interests and abilities for the underrepresented gender and the present practice of accommodating such interest. The reduction of participation opportunities for the overrepresented gender is not acceptable as it does not show good faith efforts to expand opportunities for the underrepresented gender. For prong 3, OCR reviews whether there is enough interest in a particular sport, sufficient ability of the potential participants, and reasonable expectation of competition for the team.

Regarding prong 3, in order to determine if there is sufficient interest to add a sport for the underrepresented gender, some schools have used survey instruments to collect data on student interest levels. Other schools have implemented a formal review process where students may file paperwork to request the addition of a new sport team.

NCAA's Philosophy Statement on Gender Equity. Whereas Title IX is a federal law requiring gender-equitable access and treatment as specified by regulations, the NCAA's philosophy statement on gender equity refers to the spirit of the law that colleges should strive to achieve. The terminology, developed in 1991 by the National Association of Collegiate Women Athletics Administrators leadership, appeared in the 1993 NCAA Convention proceedings and can be found today on the NCAA's Gender Equity Web page. It states: "An athletics program can be considered gender equitable when the participants in both the men's and women's sports programs would accept as fair and equitable the overall program of the other gender" (National Collegiate Athletic Association, n.d.[a]). The concept of achieving gender equity is one where male and female athletes are treated fairly and equitably.

Sport Sponsorship. In addition to understanding the letter of Title IX as well as the spirit of the NCAA's concept of gender equity, athletics decision makers must abide by applicable NCAA regulations. In order to be an NCAA Division I, II, or III member institution, certain membership requirements, including minimum sport sponsorship requirements, must be met. For example, a Division I institution must offer a minimum of seven sports for men, seven sports for women (or six sports for men and eight for women if offering football), with at least two team sports for each gender. Each playing season (fall, winter, and spring) must be represented, and a defined set of minimum contest and participant requirements as well as game scheduling criteria must be met (National Collegiate Athletic Association, 2009).

As it relates to sports sponsorship, adding or dropping sport teams will inevitably affect the male-to-female scholarship ratio. Therefore, an understanding of Title IX scholarship requirements and NCAA financial aid regulations is also imperative.

Financial Aid Restrictions. Regarding Title IX scholarship regulations, the 1998 Bowling Green "Dear Colleague Letter" from the U.S. Department of Education's OCR (U.S. Department of Education, 1998) reaffirms the federal requirement that the awarding of aid be substantially proportionate to the student athlete participation rates. This means that if men are 55 percent of the student athletes, they should receive 55 percent of the athletics aid (with a variance of 1 percent generally permitted). For an institution to be in compliance with the financial aid component, anything beyond 1 percent may be only for nondiscriminatory reasons, such as differences in out-of-state resident tuition costs. Differences cannot be due to limits on the availability of out-of-state scholarships for women.

According to NCAA rules, for each sport sponsored, there is a limit on the number of scholarships that may be offered. For purposes of awarding scholarships, the NCAA designates certain sports as "head count" sports

NEW DIRECTIONS FOR INSTITUTIONAL RESEARCH • DOI: 10.1002/ir

and others as "equivalency sports." In head count sports, no more than the designated number of individuals (head counts) may receive aid (such as twelve head count for Division I gymnastics, twelve for women's volleyball, and eight for women's tennis). In equivalency sports, the school may divide up a single scholarship among more than one athlete. Examples of Division I equivalency sports are field hockey (twelve), golf (six), lacrosse (twelve), rowing (twenty), soccer (fourteen), softball (twelve), track and field/cross country (eighteen), and swimming/diving (fourteen).

When evaluating sport sponsorship issues within an athletic program, a complex set of factors is at play. Decision makers must take into account the number of participants who may be involved, as well as the NCAA scholarship maximums to ensure that Title IX compliance in one area (participation) does not result in noncompliance in another area (scholarships). This is particularly important if an institution is considering additions or reductions to team rosters or teams sponsored by the athletic department.

Gender Equity Data and Resource Materials

A number of resources are available that can help administrators involved in discussions and deliberations regarding gender equity, sport sponsorship, and participation. These resources can help answer questions, such as: What sports should we add? How many athletes are on a typical team? How many other colleges offer the sport? What sports are gaining in popularity? What are similar schools offering? What sports are available through our high school feeder systems? What resource documents are most helpful in understanding Title IX and its application?

This section provides an overview of gender equity data and resources that are available to answer questions like the ones posed. It includes an explanation of how NCAA sports sponsorship data, the EADA tool, and High School Federation statistics can be used to improve institutional decision making.

NCAA Sports Sponsorship and Participation Rates Report. The NCAA publishes sports sponsorship and participation rates in a report it makes available on its Web site (DeHass, 2008). The report offers data on the number of teams, athletes, and average squad sizes for NCAA Divisions I, II, and III championship sports and nonchampionship sports (including emerging sports for women). Analyzing the data gives both a snapshot of current statistics and a perspective on emerging trends. For example, a snapshot of the NCAA data from the 2006–2007 year for women's sports shows that the top sport teams for women in descending order based on number of teams overall are: (1) basketball, 1,050 teams; (2) volleyball, 1,007 teams; (3) cross country teams, 967; (4) softball, 942 teams; (5) soccer, 941 teams; (6) tennis, 895 teams; (7) outdoor track, 732 teams; (8) indoor track, 641 teams; (9) swimming and diving, 504 teams; and (10) golf, 512 teams. The divisional breakdown can also be ascertained from the data.

Based on an examination of sport teams offered over the past ten years, we can see trends such as increases in select sports. In comparing the 1996–1997 year to the 2006–2007 statistics, the sport of soccer grew from 694 to 941 teams, the sport of golf grew from 303 to 512 teams, and the sport of lacrosse added over 100 teams and grew to 286. Women's rowing also expanded during this period, from 98 to 144 teams (DeHass, 2008).

In the report, the NCAA has designated certain sports as emerging sports to give greater visibility and support to help colleges achieve gender equity. For example, the sports of bowling, water polo, and ice hockey were officially identified as emerging sports, and eventually they became part of the NCAA championships, with forty-nine bowling teams, sixty-one water polo teams, and seventy-nine ice hockey teams for women by 2006–2007 (DeHass, 2008; National Collegiate Athletic Association, n.d.[b]). Some sports originally identified as emerging sports for women have not increased and therefore have been removed from the emerging sport list: archery, badminton, synchronized swimming, and team handball. The sports of equestrian, rugby, and squash still remain on the emerging sport list; and NCAA Divisions I and II institutions recently voted to add sand volleyball to the emerging sport list to be effective August 1, 2010 (National Collegiate Athletic Association, n.d.[b]).

Other championship sports have remained stagnant. For example, the number of gymnastics teams (86), fencing teams (45), and skiing teams (44) remained about the same during this ten-year period. The number of field hockey teams rose slightly, to 259 (DeHass, 2008).

In addition to knowing which sports are being added by other schools, it is helpful in the planning process to know the number of athletes who typically comprise a team. The NCAA Sports Sponsorship and Participation Rates Report (DeHass, 2008) includes data on average squad sizes per division per sport. For example, according to the 2006–2007 NCAA Division I statistics, the average women's rowing team squad size is sixty-three, the average indoor and outdoor track squad size is thirty-five to thirty-six, soccer is twenty-six, field hockey is twenty-two, and the average women's golf team comprises nine student athletes.

Equity in Athletics Disclosure Act. On an annual basis, colleges are required to submit athletics data to the U.S. Department of Education's Office of Postsecondary Education (OPE). The data are made available through OPE's database: the Equity in Athletics Data Analysis Cutting Tool (U.S. Department of Education, n.d.). The cutting tool can be used to develop customized reports on equity in athletics data. Information on one institution as well as aggregated data for a group of colleges or universities can be accessed:

- *Narrowing the search.* Decision makers can select institutions that may be similar to their own for comparison purposes because the database allows users to select one or more fields as search criteria. The fields that may be used as search criteria are locale (such as city or state), sports governing body, divisional affiliation, conference affiliation, type of institution, and size of the institution based on undergraduate enrollment numbers.

- *Available statistics.* For each collegiate institution, the following statistics are provided: undergraduate enrollment, sport participants, coaching information, and revenues and expenses.
- *Undergraduate enrollment.* For the undergraduate enrollment category, the number of full-time male and female undergraduate students attending the university is provided.
- *Sport participants.* The data provided on sports participants include the types of sports offered, number of male and female participants per sport, and total number of male and female athletes. The data for the total number of male and female participants are provided in two ways: the duplicated count, which counts an athlete once for each sport in which he or she participates, and an unduplicated count, in which the athlete counts as one regardless of whether the individual participates in more than one sport. The duplicated count is used for determining sport participation opportunities under prong 1 of the three-prong test. The unduplicated count is used for determining scholarship ratios. This means that an athlete competing in indoor track, outdoor track, and cross country would count three times for determining sport participation opportunities but only once for purposes of assessing financial aid.
- *Coaching information.* Charts are provided detailing the number of full-time and part-time head and assistant coaches per sport for each men's team and each women's team, as well as full-time, part-time, and volunteer staff. The average salaries of head coaches for men's teams and women's teams are provided, as are the average salaries for assistant coaches.
- *Financial data.* The amount of athletically related financial aid (total dollars and percentage to male and female student athletes) is provided. In addition, total revenues and expenses, as well as the breakdown by men's and women's teams for recruiting expenses, operating expenses, team expenses, and unallocated expenses, are provided. There are some limitations with the data in that the revenue figures do not indicate the sources of funding, which may include ticket sales, television revenues, or student fees.

In summary, not only can decision makers review data for their institution, but they can compare similar schools to see what sports, number of coaches, salaries, amount of recruiting expenses, and resources are typically being provided.

High School Federation Statistics. The number of sport teams and participants available at the high school level can also be used as a factor when considering what new sports to add to a program. The National Federation of State High Schools Association's Participation Figures Search survey (National Federation of State High Schools Association, n.d.) provides a history of boys' and girls' high school participation rates in particular sports, as well as the number of high schools offering the sport. National data on male and female sport participants and sport teams offered, as well as state-by-state data, are available through NFHS. According to an NFHS report fifty-five percent of high school students participated in sports in 2008–09 which is a record high (Howard and Gillis, 2009). The NFHS 2008–09 participation survey found that outdoor track and field surpassed basketball as the most popular sport for girls with 457,732 participants, followed by basketball (444,809), volleyball (404,243), fast pitch softball (368,921), soccer (344,534), cross country (198,199), tennis (177,593), swimming and diving (158,878), competitive spirit squads (117,793), and golf (69,223) (Howard and Gillis, 2009).

Other Resource Materials. Additional gender equity resources that may be useful to decision makers who are engaged in gender equity and sport sponsorship discussions can help clarify the nuances of the regulations as well as provide additional information such as start-up dollars for emerging sports.

The NCAA's Diversity and Inclusion Web site (http://www.ncaa.org/wps/ncaa?ContentID=286) contains a Title IX and Gender Equity subsection and Title IX Resource Center, with manuals, videos, Web tutorials, and other resources. The 2008 NCAA publication titled *Gender Equity in Intercollegiate Athletics: A Practical Guide for Colleges and Universities* (National Collegiate Athletic Association, 2008) is a 298-page comprehensive manual that provides an in-depth look at how Title IX applies to intercollegiate athletics and includes practical advice and real-life examples to help colleges alleviate inequalities in their intercollegiate athletics programs. See http://www.ncaapublications.com/ProductsDetailView.aspx?sku=GE2008.

A number of sources provide historical information, clarifications, and policy information. Title IX regulations, interpretations, and clarifications can be found on the Office for Civil Rights Web site at http://www.ed.gov/about/offices/list/ocr/index.html. *The Iowa Gender Equity in Sports* Web site at http://bailiwick.lib.uiowa.edu/ge/ provides historical information on Title IX, a timeline, federal and state guidelines, as well as links to other useful Web sites. *The Women's Sports Foundation* (http://www.womenssportsfoundation.org/) developed a number of policy position statements on Title IX and gender equity related topics, such as the dropping of men's sport teams.

Issues and Implications

Issues that have surfaced regarding gender equity, sport participation, and sponsorship include the dropping of sport teams, the use of interest surveys, and financial implications of sport participation decisions.

Dropping of Women's Teams. The case of *Cohen* v. *Brown* (1993) addressed Title IX compliance at Brown University after its decision to cut both men's and women's sport teams. Because the percentage of female athletes at Brown was still lower than the percentage of female undergraduates after the cuts, the institution did not satisfy the first prong (proportionality). Also, in cutting two women's sport teams, the institution no longer satisfied the second prong (history and continuing practice of program expansion for the underrepresented gender). Finally, Brown did not satisfy the third prong because it cut two viable and competitive women's teams and therefore was not considered to be "accommodating the interests and abilities of the underrepresented gender" (*Cohen v. Brown University*, 1993). The university was found not in compliance with Title IX's three-prong test for participation opportunities and was required to reinstate the women's sport teams. In summary, if women are the underrepresented gender, a college that drops a viable women's sport will most likely not be complying with Title IX's three-prong test unless the college meets proportionality (prong 1).

Use of Survey Instruments. When coupled with other data, such as high school participation rates and conference sport offerings, the use of interest surveys can serve as a helpful tool to assess levels of undergraduate student interest in select sports, particularly when considering what sports to add for the underrepresented gender.

In 2005, OCR expanded the use of interest surveys to allow schools to determine compliance based on the use of a model survey. Ongoing controversy surrounding the expanded use of interest surveys in this manner stems from the 2005 clarification, which appears to allow a loophole to circumvent the spirit of Title IX. The concern is that some schools may interpret a lack of response to an e-mail survey as a lack of interest in sports. NCAA president Myles Brand, the NCAA executive committee, and Title IX advocacy groups have advised against using interest surveys in this manner and have asked OCR to retract its 2005 clarification (Brutlag, 2006).

Unintended Financial Consequences. When adding or dropping sport teams, athletics decision makers must understand the link between sport participation and financial aid to ensure that Title IX compliance in one area (participation) does not result in noncompliance in another area (scholarships). In addition, the dropping or adding of sport teams may have unintended consequences elsewhere. For example, if an institution tiers its sport teams and drops a lower-tiered men's sport team, the treatment level of female athletes compared to male athletes needs to be reassessed and could result in the need to spend new dollars, for example, for enhancing women's sport facilities.

Conceptual Framework for Sport Sponsorship Decision Making

When working with athletics budgets, determining how to comply with Title IX and, in particular, whether to add or eliminate sport programs, there are many factors to consider. From a philosophical standpoint, it is important to review the institution's mission and the athletics department's mission, as well as to discuss with stakeholders who may be affected by a decision. A comprehensive decision-making framework can be of assistance to administrators in this process.

The responsible decision-making model for athletics (RDMMA) can be used to assist athletics decision makers when reviewing sport participation opportunities (Yiamouyiannis, Lawrence, Hums, and Ridpath, 2009). Through use of this model, the administrator would:

- Identify the specific problem
- Identify the preferred outcomes, taking into account key stakeholders and become familiar with factors internally and externally that could influence the outcome
- Review available data
- Identify potential hurdles or problem areas
- Develop and assess alternatives and then make a decision

In applying the RDMMA, the issues athletics decision makers must balance are threefold: the pressure to win in select sports, budget limitations, and the need to comply with Title IX. The goals and objectives involve the need to comply with Title IX, balance the budget, and provide competitive sport opportunities for student athletes as a function within the university. This requires a review of applicable laws and regulations; financial audits; philosophical discussions about the mission of the sports program; and the impact of potential decisions on key stakeholders, such as student athletes, students, fans, alumni, faculty, and community members. Regarding budgets, facilities and the financial impact of potential decisions should be fully considered before making final decisions. In summary, the use of a formal review process that involves key stakeholders, a review of pertinent data, and the use of resources can help ensure that the desired outcomes are achieved (Yiamouyiannis, Lawrence, Hums, and Ridpath, 2009).

Conclusion

Many challenges lay ahead for athletics decision makers who face escalating financial demands, the need to comply with Title IX requirements, and the continued pressure to win. To assist athletics administrators who may be involved in the sports sponsorship decision-making process, this chapter has described Title IX and NCAA regulations related to sport sponsorship and participation, as well as available NCAA and EADA data and uses of those data. In addition, issues such as the dropping of teams, the use of interest surveys, and unintended consequences of actions were covered. The chapter concluded with identifying and explaining a theoretical framework that can be used to aid in the decision-making process regarding gender equity, sport sponsorship and participation opportunities.

References

Brutlag, M. B. "'Lack of Interest?' College Athletics Community Stands Back from New Title IX Compliance Tool." *NCAA News*, Apr. 10, 2006. Retrieved Feb. 2, 2009, from http://www.ncaa.org/wps/ncaa?ContentID=4114.

Cohen v. Brown University. 991 F.2d 888 (1993).

DeHass, D. M. *NCAA Sports Sponsorship and Participation Rates Report, 1981–82 – 2006–07.* 2008. Retrieved Nov. 15, 2008, from http://www.ncaapublications.com/ProductsDetailView.aspx?sku=PR2008.

Howard, B., and Gillis, J. *High School Sports Participation Increases for 20th Consecutive Year.* Sept. 15, 2009. Retrieved Dec. 2, 2009, from http://www.nfhs.org/content.aspx?id=3505.

National Collegiate Athletic Association (NCAA). *Division I Manual.* 2009–2010. (2009). Retrieved Dec. 3, 2009, from http://www.ncaapublications.com/ProductsDetailView.aspx?sku=D110.

National Collegiate Athletic Association. "Gender Equity in Intercollegiate Athletics: A Practical Guide for Colleges and Universities." 2008. Retrieved Nov. 6, 2009, from http://www.ncaapublications.com/Uploads/PDF/Gender_Equity_Intercollegiate_Athleticsd6b7f57a-0db1-45fe-b4d6-7c74ed2c1350.pdf.

National Collegiate Athletic Association. "NCAA Gender Equity." Gender Equity Task Force, n.d.[a]. Retrieved Nov. 3, 2009, from http://www.ncaa.org/wps/ncaa?ContentID=286.

National Collegiate Athletic Association. "Emerging Sports for Women." n.d.[b]. Retrieved Nov. 3, 2009, from http://www.ncaa.org/wps/ncaa?ContentID=40539.

National Federation of State High Schools Association. "Participation Figures Search." n.d. Retrieved Jan. 24, 2009, from http://www.nfhs.org/custom/participation_figures/default.aspx.

Title IX and Intercollegiate Athletics: A Policy Interpretation. 44 F.R. § 239 (1979). Retrieved Nov. 21, 2006, from http://www.ed.gov/about/offices/list/ocr/docs/t9interp.html.

U.S. Department of Education. Office for Civil Rights. "Dear Colleague Letter: Bowling Green State University." July 23, 1998. Retrieved Nov. 6, 2009, from http://www.ed.gov/about/offices/list/ocr/docs/bowlgrn.html.

U.S. Department of Education. Office for Civil Rights. "Clarification of Intercollegiate Athletics Policy Guidance: The Three-Part Test." Jan 16, 1996. Retrieved Nov. 16, 2009, from http://www.ed.gov/about/offices/list/ocr/docs/clarific.html.

U.S. Department of Education. Postsecondary Education. "Equity in Athletics Data Analysis Cutting Tool." n.d. Retrieved Jan. 2, 2009, from http://ope.ed.gov/athletics/.

Yiamouyiannis, A., Lawrence, H., Hums, M., and Ridpath, D. "Use of the Responsible Decision Making Model for Athletics (RDMMA) to Address Conflicting Priorities at NCAA Division I Member Institutions." Unpublished manuscript, 2009.

ATHENA YIAMOUYIANNIS *is assistant professor of sports administration at Ohio University.*

NEW DIRECTIONS FOR INSTITUTIONAL RESEARCH • DOI: 10.1002/ir

5

Policymakers can use sport injury and exposure data to enhance the student athlete experience and make data-driven policy, rules, and equipment decisions.

Data-Driven Decision Making in Practice: The NCAA Injury Surveillance System

David Klossner, Jill Corlette, Julie Agel, Stephen W. Marshall

Putting data-driven decision making into practice requires the use of consistent and reliable data that are easily accessible. The systematic collection and maintenance of accurate information is an important component in developing policy and evaluating outcomes. Since 1982, the National Collegiate Athletic Association (NCAA) has been collecting injury and exposure data from a sample of member institutions through the Injury Surveillance System (ISS). These data inform policy decisions made by NCAA committees and external organizations charged with overseeing the health and safety of student athletes. These data also provide individual institutions with injury information for campus-based evaluations of student athletes' welfare.

The ISS example in this chapter illustrates how data-driven decision making can be applied to other aspects of intercollegiate athletics. The ISS demonstrates how elements such as variable definitions and sampling schemes are key features for developing longitudinal data sets that can be used to inform decision making and evaluate the impact of policy change. The chapter also describes the challenges and trade-offs of data collection based largely on voluntary cooperation among member institutions.

NEW DIRECTIONS FOR INSTITUTIONAL RESEARCH, no. 144, Winter 2009 © Wiley Periodicals, Inc.
Published online in Wiley InterScience (www.interscience.wiley.com) • DOI: 10.1002/ir.313

Documenting the Health and Safety of the Student Athlete Experience

The demands for information related to student athletes and intercollegiate athletics continue to grow. These demands come from faculty, the public, and governing agencies. These constituent groups may have divergent goals and agendas. Today there is also the expectation that this information will be quickly and easily accessible. Within the NCAA, the Committee on Competitive Safeguards and Medical Aspects of Sports (CSMAS) oversees the collection, maintenance, and use of complex, sophisticated injury data that inform policy related to the health and safety of the student athlete experience.

The mission of CSMAS, formed in 1958, is to provide expertise and leadership to the NCAA in order to promote a healthy and safe environment for student athletes through research, education, collaboration, and policy development. In its earliest years, the primary responsibility of CSMAS was research, mostly carried out through small grants to faculty researchers at member campuses. Many of these grants covered health and safety; catastrophic and fatal injuries, now handled through the National Center for Catastrophic Injury Research; equipment standards, more commonly handled by standards writing bodies such as the National Operating Committee on Standards for Athletic Equipment, the American Society for Testing and Materials, and the Hockey Equipment Certification Council; and sports injury surveillance. The NCAA published its first Sports Medicine Handbook in 1977, began gathering its own sport injury surveillance data in 1982, and implemented drug testing for NCAA championships in 1986.

One of the more important duties of the CSMAS has been to operate a national Injury Surveillance System (ISS) to monitor injury trends and enhance safety of student athletes participating in practice, training, and competition. The ISS was developed in 1982 to provide current and reliable data on injury trends in intercollegiate athletics. Injury and exposure data are collected yearly from a volunteer sample of sports at NCAA member institutions and the resulting data summaries are reviewed by the CSMAS, NCAA Sport Rules Committees, and many other NCAA committees interested in the well-being of student athletes. To put this in perspective, with less than a 15 percent sample of fifteen sports, the ISS system has collected data on over 180,000 injuries over sixteen years as student athletes accumulated more than 27 million practice exposures and 5 million competition exposures. The goal of the NCAA injury surveillance program continues to be using these data to monitor and reduce injury rates through suggested changes in rules, protective equipment, medical care policy, or coaching techniques. The following information regarding the ISS and its methodology is reprinted with permission from the *Journal of Athletic Training.*

NEW DIRECTIONS FOR INSTITUTIONAL RESEARCH • DOI: 10.1002/ir

NCAA Injury Surveillance System

Recognizing its organizational health and safety roots, the NCAA has maintained the ISS for intercollegiate athletics since 1982. The primary goal of the ISS is to collect injury and exposure data from a representative sample of NCAA institutions in a variety of sports. Relevant data are then shared with appropriate NCAA sport and policy committees to provide a foundation for evidence-based decision making on health and safety issues.

Study definitions for this longitudinal surveillance study are the cornerstone to the long-term success of data analysis and application. The ISS collects data on injuries and exposures that occur in organized practices and competitions from the first day of preseason to the final postseason competition. The injury and exposure variables were combined to calculate an injury rate. Definitions for reportable injuries, reportable exposures, injury rates, and seasons have been consistent, with one addition, as noted below, since the system's inception.

Injury. A reportable injury in the ISS was defined as one that:

- Occurred as a result of participation in an organized intercollegiate practice or contest *and*
- Required medical attention by a team-certified athletic trainer or physician *and*
- Resulted in restriction of the student athlete's participation or performance for one or more calendar days beyond the day of injury.

If an off day followed the injury event, athletic trainers were asked to assess whether the injured athlete would have been able to participate.

On occasion, the injury definition was expanded based on severity or significance. For example, in the 1994–1995 academic year, dental injuries were included regardless of time loss.

Exposure. A reportable athlete exposure (A-E) is defined as one student athlete participating in one practice or competition in which he or she was exposed to the possibility of athletic injury, regardless of the time associated with that participation. Only participants with actual playing time were counted as having game exposures. Preseason intrateam scrimmages were classified as practice, not competition.

Injury Rate. An injury rate is a measure of the incidence of injury, defined as the number of injuries in a particular category divided by the number of A-Es in that category. In the ISS, this value was expressed as injuries per 1,000 A-Es. For example, 6 contest injuries during 563 contest A-Es resulted in an injury rate of (6/563) (1,000, or 10.7 contest injuries/1,000 A-Es).

Seasons. The traditional sport season is used for data collection and is divided into three subcategories defined by the NCAA: preseason (full team practices and competitions before the first regular season contest), inseason (all practices and contests from the first regular season contest through the last regular season contest), and postseason (all practice and contests after the last regular season contest through the last postseason contest).

Academic Year. The academic year is defined as beginning July 1 and ending June 30.

Time Loss. Time loss is defined as the time between the original injury and return to participation at a level that would allow competition participation. Only injuries that are recorded as time loss are used as a basic marker to help isolate the injuries that are the most severe.

Sampling and Data Collection

Since 1988, the ISS has collected data from five fall sports (men's football, men's soccer, women's soccer, field hockey, and women's volleyball), six winter sports (men's basketball, women's basketball, men's ice hockey, women's gymnastics, men's gymnastics, and men's wrestling), and five spring sports (men's baseball, women's softball, men's lacrosse, women's lacrosse, and spring football). Data collection for women's ice hockey began in the 2000–2001 academic year. Individual institution sport sponsorship varies significantly within the NCAA.

Data Collection. Since 1988, schools annually participating in ISS data collection have gathered those data through their certified athletic trainers. Participation in the NCAA ISS is voluntary and available to all member institutions. Each spring, a letter requesting participation in the ISS is sent to the head athletic trainer at each NCAA member institution. Attached to each letter is a checklist of the sixteen sports covered by the ISS. The athletic training staff is asked to select one primary sport and any secondary sports for data collection in each of the three sport seasons (fall, winter, and spring).

The initial target sample is 10 percent of the schools from each of the three NCAA divisions that sponsor a particular sport. To achieve this target, all primary requests are accepted, and all secondary requests are randomly accepted until 15 percent of sponsoring schools are enlisted. This sampling scheme is used in an attempt to balance the dual needs of maintaining a reasonably representative cross-section of NCAA institutions while accommodating the needs of the voluntary participants. Thus, the group of schools contributing data is a convenience sample rather than a random sample.

Participating athletic trainers are instructed to submit data from the first day of official preseason practice to the final day of any postseason competition. No data are collected during out-of-season or nontraditional-season activities except for the well-defined maximum fifteen-day spring football practice activity.

Injury Form. A two-page injury form is completed and submitted by standard mail to the NCAA for each reportable injury. This form contains approximately thirty questions related to basic injury mechanism, when and where the injury occurred, body part injured, type of injury, measures of severity (time loss and need for surgery), and sport-specific questions (such as position played and specific injury mechanisms such as contact with a stick). If more than one body part has been injured in the same injury event, a separate form is completed for each injury. No names or other personal identification information are collected.

Exposure Form. A one-page exposure form is submitted weekly to the NCAA by each participating school. This form summarizes the number of practices and contests; the average number of participants for each activity; the season (preseason, regular season, or postseason); the type of playing surface for each activity, if relevant; and the location of the contest (home or away). Contest participants are counted only if they officially participated in some part of the contest. Exposure forms are submitted weekly, even if no injuries are reported during that time period.

Unique Challenges. Forms received by the NCAA are entered into a database created specifically for the ISS. Other than the unique school code number and sport, no identifiers are present on either the injury or exposure forms. Two weeks after the end of the NCAA championship in a given sport, each school's data are reviewed to ensure compliance with the minimum number of submitted exposure weeks for games and practices (defined as at least 70 percent of possible weeks). Schools meeting this criterion are included in the aggregate division and national samples. Each participating school in the national sample receives a hard copy of its own data, as well as copies of the appropriate division and national samples for the given academic year. A summary book containing selected injury data across all the years of data collection is distributed to participating schools for reporting basic trends. As a further participation incentive, a small monetary incentive is provided to the person in charge of data collection for each sport that qualifies to be in the national sample.

ISS Data Analysis and Presentation

In 2007, the NCAA and the National Athletic Trainers' Association partnered to publish a special issue of the *Journal of Athletic Training*, which was dedicated to the ISS data (Hootman, Covassin, and Evans, 2007). Sport-specific chapters provided a window into the types and frequencies of injuries related to athletic activity commonly reported, such as:

- *School participation frequency:* Number of schools participating in the ISS compared with all schools sponsoring the particular sport at the NCAA varsity level in each division during each academic year.
- *Average annual game and practice athlete-exposures by division:* Average number of games, game exposures, practices, and practice exposures condensed over academic years for each division.
- *Game and practice injury rates over academic years:* Game and practice injury rates over academic years (divisions combined).

- *Game and practice injury rates by division and season:* Game and practice injury rates over relevant academic years by division and season (preseason, in-season, and postseason).
- *Game and practice injury frequency by major body part:* Overall frequency for head/neck, upper extremity (includes shoulder/clavicle through fingers), trunk/back (includes pelvis, hips, groin, and internal organs), lower extremity (includes upper leg through toes), and other injuries for games and practices (academic years and divisions combined).
- *Most common game and practice injuries:* Most common body part or injury type combinations in games and practices (academic years and divisions combined). In select sports, additional figures show a more detailed analysis of injury mechanism, such as contact with ground or contact with ball. In these analyses, the injury mechanism is the action that was the primary direct contributor to the injury. For example, if someone fell due to player contact and sustained a knee abrasion from scraping the ground, the reported specific injury mechanism would be contact with the ground.
- *Game and practice injury mechanism:* Percentage of injuries in games and practices resulting from player contact, other contact, and no contact mechanisms (academic years and divisions combined).
- *Top game and practice injuries resulting in ten or more days of activity time loss:* Most common game and practice injuries restricting participation for at least ten days and most common mechanism of such injuries.
- *Additional tables and figures:* Selected sport-specific data (if applicable). These tables and figures highlight sport-specific injuries or mechanisms of interest.

The journal chapters identified several general conclusions across all sports over sixteen years (Hootman, Covassin, and Evans, 2007):

- More than half of all collegiate athletic injuries were to the lower extremities.
- Preseason practice injury rates were two to three times higher than injury rates recorded during the regular seasons.
- Competition injury rates were higher than in practice.
- Rates of concussions and anterior cruciate ligament (ACL) knee injuries increased significantly, possibly due in part to improved reporting and identification of these injuries over the collected years.
- Sports involving collision and contact, such as football and wrestling, had the highest injury rates in both games and practices. Men's baseball had the lowest rate of injuries in practice and women's softball the lowest rate in games.

Two common themes seem to suggest the need for more controlled research-oriented study:

- Competition injury rates did not change statistically over time. As the association has addressed many sport rules to minimize the risk of sport injury over the sixteen year period, this was not shown statistically.
- Sports that have rules directly limiting player contact, such as men's and women's soccer and basketball and women's ice hockey, still have a significant number of injuries caused by contact with players.

NCAA Legislation Related to Risk Minimization

The NCAA worked collaboratively with committees and external stakeholders such as the American Football Coaches Association between 2001 and 2004 on issues related to sudden death, heat illness, and preseason injury rates. This collaboration was grounded in the use of the NCAA ISS data for football that helped guide discussion and policy decisions. The result included extensive educational materials and legislative changes for the out-of-season and preseason periods. The purpose was to allow student athletes to acclimate to exercise intensity, the addition of equipment in the heat, and the environment stressors. Significant practice policy changes included, for the first time, a more regulated practice period. In football, the preseason practice now begins with a five-day acclimatization period for both first-time participants (freshmen and transfers) and continuing student athletes.

NCAA Sport Rule Modifications Related to Risk Minimization

The NCAA publishes seventeen rules books for nineteen sports (cross country, indoor track and field, and outdoor track and field are in one book) and has eighteen playing rules committees (men's and women's basketball share the same rules book but have two separate committees).

In general, a playing rules book is intended to include only those things that a game official can reasonably control. There are some cases where a rules book may be the best place to house a certain rule (such as wrestling weight management policies and procedures), but as a guiding principle, enforceability of rules for officials is key for inclusion in the rules book.

The NCAA has used the ISS aggregated data during discussions on multiple sport topics on a regular basis. Although not all discussions lead to rules changes, points of emphasis within the rules book or educational initiatives are common. Some examples of more significant rules changes include these:

- *Ice hockey (1995).* Analysis of concussion injuries in ice hockey led to rules changes and officiating emphasis on reducing hitting from behind and contact to the head in the sport.
- *Baseball (1998).* The NCAA established a woodlike standard for nonwood bats that protects the integrity of the game and the safety of the student athletes.

NEW DIRECTIONS FOR INSTITUTIONAL RESEARCH • DOI: 10.1002/ir

- *Pole vault (2002).* The NCAA Track and Field Committee implemented rules changes to minimize the risk of injury in the pole vault. Those changes included extending the landing area in the pit and adding padding around the standards.
- *Women's lacrosse (2003).* The NCAA mandated the use of appropriate eye protection in women's lacrosse to minimize the risk of catastrophic eye injury.
- *Football: Head-down contact, spearing prevention, and targeting a defense-less player (2005, 2008).* Due to concerns over continued head and neck injuries related to head-down contact and spearing in football, the NCAA Football Rules Committee changed the college football rules in 2005 and again in 2008 regarding spearing and head-down contact. In addition to the rule change, the NCAA focused on the education of student athletes, coaches, officials, and administrators regarding prevention of head and neck injuries through educational video and poster distribution.
- *Wrestling (2008).* Skin infections continue to be a concern for this close contact sport, and the ISS continues to provide data that have shown this sport injury as the number one reason student athletes are out of practice or completion. The Wrestling Rules Committee worked with the CSMAS to develop common reporting for clearance and enhanced education in an effort to reduce the risk of contracting infections.

Expanded Scope of ISS

The NCAA ISS data have influenced policy discussions outside the NCAA Governance and Sport Committee structures. Some of these involve youth sports, equipment and facilities, and medical association publications.

Youth Sports. As football has been one of the sports of highest interest, particularly preseason injuries and heat acclimatization, the ISS has helped to form preseason football acclimatization models for high school athletes (Bergeron and others, 2005). In addition, the NCAA has provided information to constituents interested in injury incidence rates. However, the ability to apply rates from ISS to other populations has been limited. The definitions established for the ISS have been used for youth sports injury surveillance programs, allowing for the comparison of similar sports between high school and collegiate athletes (Shankar and others, 2007). A main objective of injury surveillance data collection has been the ability to use longitudinal data in order to have an impact on the health and safety of student athletes. An example of the use of the NCAA data in conjunction with expert opinion is the change to mandating eyewear for protection in women's lacrosse at the high school level (Lincoln and others, 2007).

Equipment and Facilities. Injury surveillance data have enabled the NCAA and other constituent groups to examine whether the playing surface has had a role in increasing the safety of student athletes. The NCAA data have been used in two studies that looked at the role that surface played in game or practice injury rates and found, with the two years of data gathered, that there were no significant differences in injury rate between new-generation artificial turf and grass (Fuller, Dick, Corlette, and Schmalz, 2007a, 2007b). Beyond surface impact on injury rates, the use or allowed use of protective equipment has also been examined. NCAA football players have been compared with New Zealand rugby players to look at the impact of protective equipment in a full contact sport (Marshall and others, 2002). A final area of continued interest in student athlete well-being has been the noted discrepancy in ACL injuries in women compared to men in similar sporting situations (Griffin and others, 2000, 2006). The longitudinal nature of the data collected in the NCAA ISS has enabled researchers to look at incidence rates of ACL injuries in a variety of sports.

Impact for Other Associations

The NCAA has a long-standing relationship with sport governing bodies through the use of ISS aggregated data. Organizations such as US Lacrosse and its Sports Science and Safety section have evaluated injuries in the sport at the collegiate level in areas such as concussion, contact injuries, head injuries, eye injuries, and heat illness that affect the entire lacrosse community. The National Wrestling Coaches Association has created educational initiatives in the area of nutrition, weight loss, and skin infection prevention through a collaborative partnership with the NCAA and its ISS injury data. The American Football Coaches Association has taken steps to address heat stress, head and spine injuries, and other player safety rules through its partnership with the NCAA and its ISS injury data. In addition, the National Federation of State High School Association's Sports Medicine Advisory Committee has used ISS data in its work to improve the student athlete welfare for secondary schools.

Medical associations have also used and benefited from NCAA ISS data. Team physician consensus statements (Herring and others, 2007), athletic training medical care and coverage models (National Athletic Trainers' Association, 2007), and prevention policies and care strategies have all been developed over the years with the help of the NCAA and its ISS injury data. Some of these organizations are the American College of Sports Medicine, the Orthopaedic Society for Sports Medicine, the American Medical Society for Sports Medicine, and the National Athletic Trainers' Association.

Future Directions

The core purpose of the NCAA is to govern competition in a fair, safe, equitable, and sportsmanlike manner and to integrate intercollegiate athletics into higher education so that the educational experience of the student athlete is paramount. The health and safety principle of the NCAA constitution provides that each member institution is responsible for protecting the health of its participating student athletes and providing a safe environment for all of them. The ISS has evolved over the past twenty-five years from a collection of injuries that occurred during football to a well-coordinated, fifteen-sport surveillance system. In 2004, the NCAA converted the paper collection method to a Web-based injury collection system. This format allows institutions real-time access to their individual data and allows the NCAA to aggregate injury and exposure data in a more timely fashion. The electronic system expanded the scope of injury types and sport-specific variables that were recorded. These enhancements provided higher-quality data and more flexibility in data analysis.

In 2005, the ISS was expanded to cover all NCAA championship and emerging sports (including women's rugby, sand volleyball, and equestrian) as well as approximately fifty club and intramural activities. In July 2009, the injury surveillance program transitioned from the NCAA national office to the Datalys Center for Sports Injury Research and Prevention. The Datalys Center, located in Indianapolis, is a national nonprofit research center formed in conjunction with the NCAA and the American College of Sports Medicine and BioCrossroads, all part of a State of Indiana initiative to develop the life sciences. Their mission is to help organizations such as the NCAA and academic researchers conduct injury surveillance and research projects that translate information into better prevention, public health, and sports medicine outcomes.

The ISS system described in this chapter demonstrates how the demands for documentation coupled with longitudinal data on the student athlete experience inform decision making among stakeholders within the NCAA and its member institutions. For example, institutional researchers and athletics administrators working with other measures of the student athlete experience such as medical insurance, injury rates, and athletic training or sports medicine costs can make data-based equipment, staffing, and facilities decisions. Decision makers have specific information needs that can be met only by longitudinal data that are consistent and easily accessed in systems like the ISS.

References

Bergeron, M. F., and others. "Youth Football: Heat Stress and Injury Risk." *Medicine and Science in Sports and Exercise*, 2005, 37(8), 1421–1430.

Fuller, C. W., Dick, R. W., Corlette, J., and Schmalz, R. "Comparison of the Incidence, Nature and Cause of Injuries Sustained on Grass and New Generation Artificial Turf by Male and Female Football Players. Part 1: Match Injuries." *British Journal of Sports Medicine*, 2007a, 41(1), 20–26.

Fuller, C. W., Dick, R. W., Corlette, J., and Schmalz, R. "Comparison of the Incidence, Nature and Cause of Injuries Sustained on Grass and New Generation Artificial Turf by Male and Female Football Players. Part 2: Training Injuries." *British Journal of Sports Medicine*, 2007b, 41(1), 27–32.

Griffin, L. Y., and others. "Noncontact Anterior Cruciate Ligament Injuries: Risk Factors and Prevention Strategies." *Journal of the American Academy of Orthopaedic Surgeons*, 2000, 8(3), 141–50.

Griffin, L. Y., and others. "Understanding and Preventing Noncontact Anterior Cruciate Ligament Injuries: A Review of the Hunt Valley II Meeting, January 2005." *American Journal of Sports Medicine*, 2006, 34(9), 1512–1532.

Herring, S. A., and others. "Selected Issues in Injury and Illness Prevention and the Team Physician: A Consensus Statement." *Medicine and Science in Sports and Exercise*, 2007, 39(11), 2058–2068.

Hootman, J. M., Covassin, T. and Evans, T. A. (eds.). "National Collegiate Athletic Association Injury Surveillance Summary for 15 Sports, 1988–1989 Through 2003–2004." *Journal of Athletic Training*, 2007, 42(2), 173–319.

Lincoln, A. E., and others. "Head, Face, and Eye Injuries in Scholastic and Collegiate Lacrosse: A 4-Year Prospective Study." *American Journal of Sports Medicine*, 2007, 35(2), 207–215.

Marshall, S. W., and others. "An Ecologic Study of Protective Equipment and Injury in Two Contact Sports." *International Journal of Epidemiology*, 2002, 31(3), 587–592.

National Athletic Trainers' Association. "Recommendations and Guidelines for Appropriate Medical Coverage of Intercollegiate Athletics." Dallas, Tex.: National Athletic Trainers' Association, 2007.

Shankar, P. R., and others. "Epidemiology of High School and Collegiate Football Injuries in the United States, 2005–2006." *American Journal of Sports Medicine*, 2007, 35(8), 1295–1303.

DAVID KLOSSNER *is the director of health and safety at the National Collegiate Athletic Association.*

JILL CORLETTE *is the director of research data, at the Datalys Center for Sports Injury Research and Prevention in Indianapolis, Indiana.*

JULIE AGEL *is a research coordinator in the Department of Orthopedic Surgery at the University of Minnesota.*

STEPHEN W. MARSHALL *is an associate professor in the Department of Epidemiology at the University of North Carolina at Chapel Hill.*

6

The College Sports Project is designed to gather data on athletics at Division III colleges and universities to inform presidents about the academic experiences of student athletes.

College Athletics and Student Achievement: The Evidence at Small Colleges

John Emerson, Rachelle L. Brooks, Elaine Croft McKenzie

Claims for the intrinsic value of intercollegiate athletics reflect the following longstanding ideals:

- "Games" are a source of pleasure and satisfaction and an important way of introducing balance into a student's life.
- By competing, one learns life lessons: teamwork, discipline, resilience, perseverance, how to play by the rules, and how to accept outcomes one may not like.
- At their best, athletic programs contribute to school spirit, help build community, and provide valuable learning opportunities.

Although one finds similar sentiments at colleges and universities at all levels, it is arguably within the NCAA Division III that claims for the educational value of athletic participation are most clearly and forcefully articulated.

Unfortunately, there exists little systematic evidence about the extent to which the realities mirror the ideals. The preponderance of attention to and research about athletics has focused on NCAA Division I institutions, even though leaders across the spectrum of higher education value data about athletics. At Division III institutions, many questions about athletic

NEW DIRECTIONS FOR INSTITUTIONAL RESEARCH, no. 144, Winter 2009 © Wiley Periodicals, Inc.
Published online in Wiley InterScience (www.interscience.wiley.com) • DOI: 10.1002/ir.314

programs remain. For example, do athletes have academic records comparable to the larger student body, and are recruited athletes performing as well in the classroom as one would expect?

A survey by the NCAA Division III Presidents Council finds that 95 percent of Division III institutions agree that student athletes should be recruited with, and perform at, the same academic standards as the general student body (National Collegiate Athletic Association Division III Presidents Council, 2008). However, research suggests that at many colleges, the relationship between intercollegiate athletics and academic values is not always harmonious (Aries and others, 2004; Fried, 2007). High-intensity, narrowly focused athletic programs can distort the experiences of student athletes and threaten the educational missions of colleges and universities. *The Game of Life* (Shulman and Bowen, 2001) and *Reclaiming the Game* (Bowen and Levin, 2003) identified disturbing trends toward greater differences between college athletes and other students in their academic achievement, choice of majors, and involvement in other aspects of collegiate life.

To build on these prior studies, the Andrew W. Mellon Foundation funded the College Sports Project (CSP) in 2003 to focus on academics and athletics within Division III. The CSP includes a longitudinal data collection effort comparing athletes to nonathletes at over eighty Division III institutions in the United States.

This chapter draws on the CSP to highlight the challenges small colleges face when collecting data about athletics and academics and uses CSP analyses to illustrate the ways these data provide a comparative assessment of athletes' academic outcomes. These examples may also suggest the limitations of any single data collection effort, no matter how comprehensive, for explaining the multiple and varied educational experiences and academic performance of student athletes. As a backdrop for the discussion of the CSP, we summarize some distinguishing characteristics of Division III and its philosophies regarding academics and athletics.

Division III Versus Division I in the NCAA

The NCAA Division III had 444 member institutions in 2008; one-fifth of these were universities and the remainder, colleges. The enrollment at these institutions averages around 2,250 students, and this modest size means that intercollegiate athletes typically comprise from one-fifth to one-third of their student bodies. In sharp contrast, athletes are a very small fraction of the student body at some of the largest institutions within Division I, such as Ohio State University and Michigan State University, both with total enrollments of over 40,000. Ethnic diversity is yet another point of contrast. At many Division I institutions, the ratio of minority athletes to minority students is very high (Lederman, 2008), whereas at many Division III institutions, athletic programs are less diverse than the student population as a whole (Fried, 2007).

NEW DIRECTIONS FOR INSTITUTIONAL RESEARCH • DOI: 10.1002/ir

Differences in philosophies about who plays sports, in which contexts, and to what ends further differentiate athletics at Division I and Division III institutions. Bowen and Levin (2003) provide a succinct description of the dissimilarities, of which the absence of athletic scholarships at Division III institutions is among the most important (National Collegiate Athletic Association, 2007a). Instead, these institutions commonly award financial aid based on need or academic merit. In addition, public spectator-oriented, income-producing athletic contests are a phenomenon of Division I institutions; within Division III the primary audiences are internal to the institution and local community, and competitions are not designed to generate revenue. The positive impact of sports on student athletes is considered especially important across Division III, and broad student participation is encouraged through the sponsorship of a maximum number and variety of athletics opportunities.

Although financial and operational distinctions between the two divisions are evident, both divisions can benefit from the availability of data on athletics. The NCAA has collaborated with other groups to produce a uniform data-reporting system for Division I that would provide dashboard indicators for peer comparisons of athletic spending (National Collegiate Athletic Association, 2007b). Although the CSP does not directly address athletic spending, its underlying motivation to provide better comparative data to presidents, the ultimate decision makers about athletics, is consistent with the NCAA's motivation to develop financial indicators at Division I institutions. Both projects promote collaboration and sharing of data among athletics, financial and academic departments, and college presidents. However, because athletics budgets at Division III are established through the same procedures that set budgets for other campus programs and units, money has a much smaller role in athletics than it does at the Division I institutions (Wesibrod, Asch and Balloou, 2008).

Common values and characteristics within Division III should not overshadow its diversity. Some of its colleges are nationally ranked and among the most highly selective in the country, whereas others admit nearly all of their qualified applicants. Most of these institutions are coeducational, but a handful have a long tradition of being single-sex colleges. Some have strong religious affiliations, whereas for others, such a connection is mostly a historical artifact.

Perhaps the most significant aspect of diversity within Division III, at least with regard to data collection about athletics, is the variation in recruiting practices for athletes. In some cases, coaches and athletics staff members work closely with admissions officers to ensure that especially talented recruits are admitted. At other institutions, admissions staff see nothing in an applicant's file to indicate he or she is being recruited by someone in athletics. This distinction, pertaining to the blindness of the admissions process for student athletes, is important, especially when information about recruitment is an integral part of a data set, as it is for the CSP. However, before turning to these and other study details, several terms and guiding principles require definition.

The Goal of "Representativeness"

The notion that athletes should be similar to the nonathletes at their respective institutions, especially in regard to their academic outcomes and opportunities for engagement in campus activities, has been a guiding principle explicitly articulated by many Division III athletic conferences (Bowen and Levin, 2003). Athletes live in the same residence halls with nonathletes, take the same courses, eat in the same dining halls, and ideally should be similar to other students in their academic motivation, interests, classroom contributions, and achievement. In short, athletes should be "representative" of their own student bodies. Underlying this concept are the principles that athletes are first and foremost students and that academic missions should not be compromised for the sake of winning athletic records.

Documenting progress toward the goal of representativeness requires the collection and dissemination of information about student academic performance—measuring and reporting on student outcomes. In recent years, state and national higher education governing bodies have asserted a need for greater measurement of accountability indicators in order to judge the quality and effectiveness of institutions. They shine a spotlight on the limited measurement of quantifiable undergraduate student outcomes and urge more systematic assessment (Brooks, 2005). The lack of innovation and interinstitutional collaboration in measuring student learning and progress greatly limits the alternatives for judging representativeness, especially in a comparative framework across Division III institutions. The CSP works within this limited landscape to leverage available data and inform conversations about the impact of athletics on educational outcomes.

Overview of the College Sports Project

The CSP is a loose confederation of around eighty institutions from NCAA Division III. One goal of the project is to provide summary data and useful information for institutional presidents interested in ensuring good alignment between their academic missions and intercollegiate athletics. A second component of the project develops programs aimed at integrating athletics more fully into the academic life of the institutions.

Building on Prior Research. The CSP was framed as a research tool to enable presidents and athletic conference heads to work collaboratively to develop local responses for slowing, and eventually reversing, any undesirable trends that might be uncovered within Division III. The project was conceived largely in response to the findings reported in *The Game of Life* (Shulman and Bowen, 2001) and, especially, *Reclaiming the Game* (Bowen and Levin, 2003) that Division III was not immune to some difficulties long associated with Division I athletics. These studies identified trends toward greater differences in admissions standards and academic outcomes between recruited athletes and nonathletes.

Other studies have found mixed trends in the differences between recruited athletes and nonathletes. A Wabash College inquiry found that among eleven liberal arts colleges, the academic performance and graduation rates of athletes were similar to or higher than their nonathlete counterparts, even when their high school performance and test scores were lower (Blaich, 2003). Similarly, Aries and colleagues (2004) discovered that when race, gender, and SAT scores were controlled for, athletic participants at two highly selective institutions did not have significantly different grade point averages (GPAs) from their nonathlete peers.

The complex relationships among academic performance, athletic status, and race have also been studied. Ethnic diversity and equality are high priorities at many institutions, as is the academic success of underrepresented minority groups. Still, Schulman and Bowen (2001) report that racial minorities who are recruited as athletes have average high school credentials that are significantly worse than those of nonrecruited students. A study by Matheson (2007) finds that in Division I, although male athletes in general graduate at a lower rate than nonathletes, male athletes within some racial/ethnic groups graduate at much higher rates than nonathletes. It is unclear whether these findings would persist in Division III or if the relationships among these factors are even more complex.

The CSP Data Collection. The CSP tracks entire entering cohorts of student athletes and nonathletes, and transfer students—from the point of admission up to graduation or withdrawal from college. It gathers demographic and secondary school data, as well as information about college athletic participation and academic performance. With data on approximately forty-four thousand students per entering cohort, the project expects to track five cohorts through at least 2011.

The data collection was designed for long-term utility, so researchers link it to other national data sets on college students using information within individual student records. For example, information about individual high schools has been attached to records from the College Board to gain a limited sense of the academic quality of high schools. Linkages to other information about students, such as postcollege educational and career plans, may identify other similarities and differences between athletes and nonathletes.

Strict confidentiality requirements, such as those set forth in the Family Educational Rights and Privacy Act, must be adhered to when undertaking any project of this type and scope. The risks associated with collecting and maintaining educational data about individual students cannot be overstated. The CSP spent many months ensuring that both project personnel and procedures comply fully with privacy and security needs.

NEW DIRECTIONS FOR INSTITUTIONAL RESEARCH • DOI: 10.1002/ir

Participating institutions have found the process of assembling CSP data challenging because of the many different locations on campuses where the information may exist. Registrars, admissions officers, athletics staff, and institutional research officers have all had a role in compiling reports for the CSP. Unfortunately records about the recruitment of student athletes are often not preserved by coaches or admissions staff in an electronic form, or even at all. Initially, paper records or the memory of athletics staff was relied on for reporting. At many institutions, the project has led to more and better record keeping and has occasionally been used as leverage for obtaining resources to improve data storage and reporting capabilities.

The practical resource constraints of those with responsibilities for CSP data collection and submission are not limited to technical and computing infrastructure. The human resources available for institutional research are generally very modest within Division III; it is not uncommon for one or two individuals on campus to perform all the internal and external reporting requirements for the college. However, because the project has instituted few changes to the data submission requirements from year to year, individuals have been able to create reporting templates to ease the data collection burden associated with the project.

A Nonprescriptive Analytical Approach. To establish trust and credibility for the project, the CSP determined it would report information directly to the presidents of participating institutions. When possible, it provides a comparative context for the data—comparison either across cohorts or with groups of other participating institutions. The CSP does not suggest how presidents should view or respond to their reports. Rather it presumes that they and other leaders are better positioned to interpret and respond as they see fit.

Illustration of CSP Findings That Inform Leaders

The following example illustrates how this data collection, analysis, and reporting mechanism has yielded findings about athletes that underscore the diversity within Division III. It also exemplifies the kinds of information that the project provides to its participating institutions, with the important difference that data given here do not include any parallel results for the local institutions.

Group Differences in Grade Point Average. The research findings in this section derive from preliminary analyses of college GPAs for a single student cohort after two years of college. Among the seventy-seven institutions contributing data for the student cohort entering college in the 2005–2006 academic year, sixty-three institutions were liberal arts colleges with data on those variables needed for the analyses. Because differences in GPAs between athletes and nonathletes are greater at more highly selective colleges, we used institutional standardized test score averages to partition these colleges into three groups: twenty-five colleges that are highly selective, twenty-three that are moderately highly selective, and fifteen that are relatively less selective in admitting students.

NEW DIRECTIONS FOR INSTITUTIONAL RESEARCH • DOI: 10.1002/ir

**Table 6.1. Average GPA Two Years After Entering
a Liberal Arts College, by Selectivity Level**

Student Group	Highly Selective	Moderately Selective	Less Selective
Male nonathlete	3.21	2.97	2.74
Male recruited	3.02	2.82	2.65
Male nonrecruited	3.15	2.89	2.75
Female nonathlete	3.34	3.21	3.02
Female recruited	3.24	3.18	3.03
Female nonrecruited	3.30	3.20	3.00

Table 6.1 gives the average GPAs for each of six student groups at the three categories of colleges. Students are classified as nonathletes if they are not recruited athletes when admitted and have never played an intercollegiate sport in college. Recruited athletes are those identified by coaches as promising athletes and are either recommended for admission or encouraged by the coaches to attend that college. Nonrecruited athletes include those students sometimes referred to as "walk-ons."

In general, male recruited athletes have lower GPAs than nonrecruited males and male nonathletes, with the greatest differences observed at the colleges with the highest selectivity. A similar pattern appears for female recruited athletes, but only at the two highest selectivity levels.

At many selective colleges and universities, an applicant's promise as an intercollegiate athlete can substantially boost the chances for that student's admittance. This indicates that standardized test scores, high school grades, and other measures of academic strength may, on average, be lower for the recruited athletes at an institution than for their nonathlete counterparts. These differences might explain why college grades and possibly other measures of achievement during college are lower for recruited athletes than for nonathletes (as observed in Table 6.1).

The Meaning and Measurement of Underperformance. When college athletes do less well than standardized test scores, high school grades, other academic indicators, and known demographic characteristics (such as gender, race/ethnicity, citizenship, and high school attended) predict, we say that they have underperformed. In particular, the difference between the college GPA for a group of athletes and the GPA for a hypothetical group of nonathletes having precisely the same known characteristics as the athlete group is a measure of the underperformance of the athletes.

To calculate underperformance, the CSP used regression models to predict GPAs based on student characteristics (see Figure 6.1). The predictor variables were demographics (gender, race/ethnicity, citizenship), measures of high school quality (such as the percentage of students from a high school planning to attend a four-year college, which was acquired from the

NEW DIRECTIONS FOR INSTITUTIONAL RESEARCH • DOI: 10.1002/ir

Figure 6.1. Variables Used in Regression Analysis to Calculate Underperformance

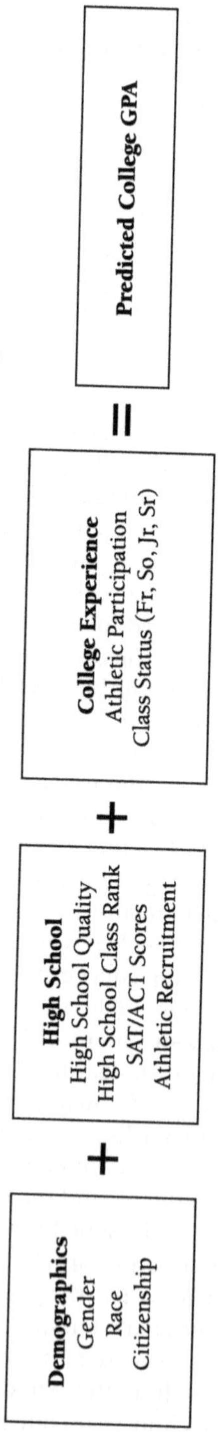

| **Demographics**
Gender
Race
Citizenship | + | **High School**
High School Quality
High School Class Rank
SAT/ACT Scores
Athletic Recruitment | + | **College Experience**
Athletic Participation
Class Status (Fr, So, Jr, Sr) | = | **Predicted College GPA** |

College Board), high school class rank, combined reading and math SAT scores (with ACT scores converted to SAT equivalents), athletic recruitment status (nonrecruited athlete, recruited athlete), college athletic participation (membership on an athletic team), and college class status (freshman, sophomore, junior, senior). The regression models predicted what the GPAs for student athletes would be if they were not athletes; that is, the model predicted GPAs based on students' academic and other characteristics, except for their athletic status. In other words, in order to understand how being a recruited athlete affects academic performance, the model estimated what students' GPAs would have been had their GPAs not been influenced by athletic participation or recruitment. For the three groups of institutions, the model predicted between 35 and 47 percent of the variation in college GPA, with higher predictive values for the less selective colleges.

Figure 6.2 displays the differences in the average college GPAs for four groups of athletes at the twenty-five most highly selective colleges. The figure also displays the predicted values of the GPA differences if athletic participation had not been a factor. The difference between these average predicted values for athletes and the actual average GPAs of the same athletes is the amount of underperformance for each athlete group, displayed as the right-most bar in each group. The differences in GPA between recruited athletes and nonathletes are greater than those between the two groups of athletes, a finding that holds for both genders. Overall, male athletes are less representative of their student bodies than are female athletes. Much of the difference in outcomes between athletes and nonathletes is attributable to underperformance, especially for the recruited athletes.

The corresponding analyses (Emerson and Brooks, 2009) for the groups of middle- and lower-selectivity colleges indicate that the differences between athletes and nonathletes typically decrease as the level of selectivity decreases. For the fifteen colleges with lower selectivity, only the male recruited athletes differ noticeably from their nonathlete counterparts, and there is little or no evidence of academic underperformance in any of the four groups of athletes. In other words, at less selective institutions, athletes are achieving at or close to the level predicted for their achievement given their entering characteristics and educational qualifications.

Explanations for Underperformance. If academic underperformance by athletes is, by definition, not explained by the observed characteristics of students when they begin college, then what is the source of underperformance? Some have speculated that the time college athletes commit to practice, training, travel, and competition could lead to lower-than-expected academic performances. However, a close look at out-of-season athletes and other students with very heavy extracurricular demands suggests that time devoted to sports cannot account for underperformance (Aries and others, 2004; Bowen and Levin, 2003). It is possible that some important cognitive or behavioral differences between recruited athletes and nonathletes may not be fully captured by test scores, high school grades, the quality of the

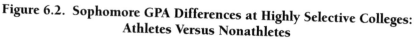

Figure 6.2. Sophomore GPA Differences at Highly Selective Colleges: Athletes Versus Nonathletes

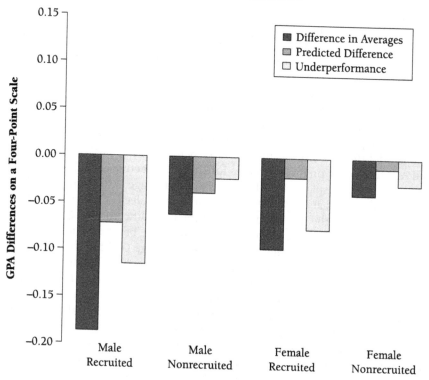

Note: Twenty-five colleges were in the sample.

high school attended, or other variables measured before students begin college. For example, academic motivation and level of interest in the college curricula may differ if recruited athletes feel an especially strong obligation to their coaches and teammates and consequently are less committed to their studies than their classmates are.

Another hypothesis is that athletes may believe, perhaps subconsciously, that others view them as being less able or less engaged in their academic pursuits, which may produce anxiety that results in lowered academic achievement. This phenomenon is what Steele (1997) referred to as "stereotype threat" and is described by Thomas Dee (2009), a Swarthmore College economist, as referring "to the perceived risk of confirming, through one's behavior or outcomes, negative stereotypes that are held about one's social identity. More specifically, its key conjecture is that the threat of being

NEW DIRECTIONS FOR INSTITUTIONAL RESEARCH • DOI: 10.1002/ir

viewed through the lens of a negative stereotype can create an anxiety that disrupts cognitive performance and influences outcomes and behaviors" (p. 1).

Dee (2009) tested the hypothesis that stereotype threat may contribute to academic underperformance by intercollegiate athletes at selective colleges. With blinded and controlled experiments, he produced evidence of stereotype threat among college athletes in a laboratory setting. His work established that stereotype threat could be a contributing factor in academic underperformance by athletes, but the extent to which this experimental finding translates into the actual experiences of athletes is still unknown.

Other Findings and Evidence for Optimism

Other empirical evidence from the CSP lends support to the attainability of the goal of athletes being representative of other students. Three general findings stand out in this regard:

1. Even at the most selective colleges, where differences in academic outcomes between athletes and nonathletes are greatest, athletes who are not recruited perform nearly as well as nonathletes.
2. When individual sports are examined, some athletes attain academic outcomes comparable to or better than those of their nonathlete classmates. (For men, these sports are cross country, indoor track, outdoor track, squash, and tennis, and for women they are cross country, indoor track, outdoor track, golf, and sailing.)
3. At many individual colleges, including some that are highly selective, athletes perform as well academically as nonathletes.

While some may believe the goal of representativeness is unattainable idealism, data from the CSP strengthen the position of college leaders who are working toward achieving greater representativeness among their intercollegiate athletes. Academic underperformance by athletes is not inevitable at Division III institutions, and it is up to institutional leaders to ensure that their academic missions are not casualties of the competitive pressures often present in the athletic arenas.

References

Aries, D., and others. "A Comparison of Athletes and Non-Athletes at Highly Selective Colleges: Academic Performance and Personal Development." *Research in Higher Education*, 2004, 45(6), 577–602.

Blaich, C. "What Kind of Game Are We Playing?" *Liberal Arts Online*, 2003, 3(11). Retrieved Mar. 1, 2009, from http://www.wabash.edu/cila/home.cfm?news_id=1386.

Bowen, W. G., and Levin, S. A. *Reclaiming the Game: College Sports and Educational Values*. Princeton, N.J.: Princeton University Press, 2003.

Brooks, R. L. "Measuring University Quality." *Review of Higher Education*, 2005, 29(1), 1–21.

Dee, T. S. "Stereotype Threat and the Student-Athlete." NBER Working Paper, No. 14075. Cambridge, Mass.: National Bureau of Economic Research, Feb. 2009.

Emerson, J. D., and Brooks, R. L. "Athletics and Academics at NCAA Division III Institutions: Data, Dialogue, and Decision-Making." Paper presented at the Annual Meeting of the American Association of Colleges and Universities: Global Challenges, College Learning, and America's Promise, Seattle, Wash., Jan. 23, 2009. http://www.aacu.org/meetings/annualmeeting/AM09/documents/CollegeSportsProject.pdf.

Fried, B. H. "Punting Our Future: College Athletics and Admissions." *Change*, June 2007, 39(3), 8–15.

Lederman, D. "Diversifying Through Football." *Inside Higher Ed*, Jan. 2008. Retrieved Mar. 7, 2009, from http://www.insidehighered.com/layout/set/print/news/2008/01/11/black.

Matheson, V. "Research Note: Athletic Graduation Rates and Simpson's Paradox." *Economics of Education Review*, 2007, 26, 516–520.

National Collegiate Athletic Association. "What's the Difference Between Divisions I, II, and III?" Feb. 1, 2007. 2007a. Retrieved Feb. 18, 2009, from http://www.ncaa.org/wps/ncaa?ContentID=418.

National Collegiate Athletic Association. "Division I Budget Trends Get Dashboard Treatment." Oct. 22, 2007. 2007b. Retrieved Feb. 5, 2009, from http://ncaawcmrun.ncaa.org:9081/wps/wcm/connect/NCAA/NCAA+News/NCAA+News+Online/2007/Division+I/Division+I+budget.

National Collegiate Athletic Association Division III Presidents Council. "Key Issues Related to the Growth of Division III: Issue Seven: Academic Considerations." White Paper, Sept. 15, 2008. Retrieved Feb. 14, 2009, from http://www.ncaa.org/wps/ncaa?ContentID=42241.

Shulman, J., and Bowen, W. G. *The Game of Life: College Sports and Educational Values.* Princeton, N.J.: Princeton University Press, 2001.

Steele, C. M. "A Threat in the Air: How Stereotypes Shape Intellectual Test Performance of African Americans." *American Psychologist*, 1997, 52(6), 613–629.

Wesibrod, B., Asch, M., and Balloou, J. *Mission and Money: Understanding the University.* Cambridge: Cambridge University Press, 2008.

JOHN EMERSON *is the Charles A. Dana Professor of Mathematics at Middlebury College and serves as principal investigator for the College Sports Project, Representativeness of Athletes.*

RACHELLE L. BROOKS *is director of the Center for Data Collection and Analysis, College Sports Project, and acting director of analytical studies at Northwestern University.*

ELAINE CROFT MCKENZIE *is a Ph.D candidate at Northwestern University and a staff analyst at the Center for Data Collection and Analysis, College Sports Project, Northwestern University.*

NEW DIRECTIONS FOR INSTITUTIONAL RESEARCH • DOI: 10.1002/ir

7

This chapter describes how the NCAA uses academic data on high school and college student athletes and the national policies that have been framed by these data.

The Collection and Use of Academic Outcomes Data by the NCAA

Todd A. Petr, Thomas S. Paskus

Although the role of academics among college students participating in intercollegiate athletics competition has been an enduring theme throughout the National Collegiate Athletic Association's (NCAA) one-hundred-year-plus history (Crowley, 2006), the NCAA has engaged in an extensive compilation of academic outcomes data on its member institutions and student athletes for only the past two decades. There are many reasons for the recent movement to collect such data, including the ease with which they can now be gathered (for example, over the Internet) and the trend toward increased reliance on data for making significant policy decisions in higher education generally (see Jenkins, 2008). A number of influences specific to college athletics could also be cited for their impact in the NCAA membership's desire to collect academic data (for example, the enhanced role of college presidents in NCAA governance), but the primary catalyst was arguably the 1983 passage of NCAA legislation commonly referred to as Proposition 48.

That legislation, which was implemented in Division I in 1986 (similar rules went into effect in Division II beginning in 1988), required that a student athlete achieve a minimum high school grade point average (GPA) in a set of core academic courses and a prescribed minimum SAT or ACT score in order to be eligible to compete in athletics as a college freshman. This was not the NCAA's first involvement in setting national academic standards, but it was the most aggressive and controversial (Crowley, 2006). Difficult questions were soon being asked by many groups. Why did the

NEW DIRECTIONS FOR INSTITUTIONAL RESEARCH, no. 144, Winter 2009 © Wiley Periodicals, Inc.
Published online in Wiley InterScience (www.interscience.wiley.com) • DOI: 10.1002/ir.315

NCAA choose these particular minimums on high school GPA and the ACT/SAT? Does the test score standard unfairly affect racial/ethnic minority student athletes and student athletes from disadvantaged backgrounds? Will these standards lead to improved college success for student athletes? In time, the NCAA membership realized they did not have sufficient data to answer those questions directly, leading to a gradual institutionalization of specific data reporting requirements of all Division I and II schools.

Today student athlete academic performance is a major focus for the NCAA and its governance structure in Divisions I and II. In Division I alone, since the passage of Proposition 48, initial academic eligibility standards have been modified on several occasions, strict progress toward degree standards have been put in place, and the academic behavior of every team is assessed, with penalties attached to poor squad performance. In contrast to the 1980s, the NCAA today compiles national data on aggregate academic performance of teams (graduation rates and academic progress rates) and conducts longitudinal cohort research that follows student athletes from high school, through college, to graduation and beyond. Taken together, these represent the most comprehensive portfolio of data on the academic trajectories of student athletes (and among the largest on college students generally) available in the United States.

This chapter describes the primary academic data collections undertaken by the NCAA (described in capsule form in Table 7.1), details the contexts related to their development, illustrates how the data are actually collected, and highlights ways in which the data have been used to create NCAA policy. We focus primarily on data from three reporting initiatives: graduation rates data, data on high school academic performance of prospective student athletes, and data on college academic performance of student athletes.

Graduation Rates Data

In January 1990, the NCAA membership passed legislation that mandated for the first time the collecting and public reporting of student athlete graduation rate data. The legislation required that the report include rates at each college or university disaggregated by race and gender and reported separately for a few specific sports teams (men's football, basketball, baseball, and track/cross country; women's basketball and track/cross country). The final methodology for calculating the graduation rates was adopted from the federal Student Right-to-Know Act, which was working its way through Congress at the time and was eventually passed in November 1990 (requiring that student athlete graduation rates be published). Under this federal formula, cohorts must consist of only first-time full-time freshmen matriculating in a given fall term while receiving athletically related financial aid. Student athletes not receiving such aid at entry and those who transfer to the institution are not included in the cohort. Transfers out of

Table 7.1. Summary of Major NCAA Division I Academic Data Collections

Data Collection	Description	Years	Predecessors
NCAA federal graduation rates data	Six-year graduation rates of scholarship freshmen student athletes and student bodies at NCAA member institutions	1984 Freshmen to the present	
NCAA Graduation Success Rate Data	Six-year graduation rates of student athletes that account for transfer students (both into and out of institutions), midyear enrollees, and some nonscholarship athletes	1995 Freshmen to the present	
NCAA Eligibility Center Data	High school transcript data on all prospective student athletes at Division I and II institutions	1994 to the present	Initial-Eligibility Clearinghouse (IEC)
Academic Performance Program Data	Term-by-term college transcript data for all scholarship student athletes in Division I	2003 to the present	Academic Performance Study (APS) Academic Performance Census (APC)

any school are considered academic failures according to this methodology. Student athletes are followed at that institution of entry for up to six years from initial enrollment, and anyone in this cohort who does not complete his or her degree by this time is considered an academic failure.

The collection of this NCAA federal graduation rate was initiated with the 1984 entering class of Division I student athletes (Division II began with the 1991 entering cohort). Because the federal government still computes overall university graduation rates using this methodology, the NCAA continues to this day to calculate the rate to serve as the primary national comparison of academic outcomes for student athletes and the general student bodies of member institutions. Over time, however, consensus grew among university presidents and chancellors that the 1990 federal methodology did not present a complete picture of how well colleges are educating student athletes or, as Adelman (2007) has shown, for the general student body. A chief concern was the way that the 1990 federal methodology treats students who transfer between institutions. Data from the U.S. Department of Education show that over 50 percent of all U.S. bachelor's degree recipients are attending more than one undergraduate institution (two-year or

NEW DIRECTIONS FOR INSTITUTIONAL RESEARCH • DOI: 10.1002/ir

four-year) prior to obtaining their degree (Adelman, 1999). Similarly, NCAA data indicate that approximately 35 percent of all scholarship student athletes in Division I have transferred into or out of their current school at some time in the six-year period after their initial enrollment in college. Under the federal methodology, transfers in or out who eventually graduate can never be counted as academically successful at any college or university. At the same time, colleges are not held accountable for any transfers in who do not graduate; for schools with high proportions of transfers in their student athlete or student body population, the federal metric potentially accounts for only a small proportion of the students actually attending the school. The federal rate has some utility as described, but it does propagate a static model of college completion that is of questionable validity today.

NCAA leaders desired to create a more dynamic or student-centered rate (one that accounts for student movement from school to school) that could be calculated using institution-level aggregate data rather than individual-level longitudinal data (which would have necessitated assignment of a student identifier and establishment of a longitudinal tracking system for student athletes). Crafting such a formula using aggregate data presented challenges, but NCAA research staff and governance committees developed such a rate. This led to the adoption of NCAA legislation that added a second graduation rate calculation to the annual reporting process beginning in 2005 (in that first year, data were collected for four separate cohorts of student athletes, with data on an additional cohort reported each fall thereafter). This second rate is called the Graduation Success Rate (GSR) in Division I and the Academic Success Rate (ASR) in Division II. Our experience has been that college presidents, faculty, and administrators overwhelmingly prefer the GSR/ASR methodology to the federal one. Efforts have been made to collaborate with the federal government on having such a rate required of colleges for their students generally, but as others have commented (Adelman, 2007), there has been little movement within the U.S. Department of Education to modernize their formula.

The definition of the cohorts for the GSR and ASR begins with the inclusion of the group of students who define the cohort using the 1990 federal methodology. In addition, a cohort includes transfers from two-year or four-year colleges who receive athletics aid on entry and freshmen on aid who first enroll at midyear. At Division I colleges that do not offer athletics-related financial aid and are thus exempt from reporting the federal rate (primarily Ivy League schools and the military academies), the GSR cohort definition is modified to replace students on athletics aid with recruited student athletes. Division II has customized the ASR to include students not receiving athletics aid, in recognition of the high percentage of Division II student athletes who fall into this category.

Transfer out of a school is somewhat more difficult to account for using aggregate data. In the GSR and ASR calculations, students in poor academic standing (defined as not being academically eligible for athletics competition had they remained at the institution) at the time of departure are counted as academic failures, while those departing in good academic standing are removed from the cohort completely (that is, they are treated as neither a success nor a failure but rather as if they were never in the cohort). The effect of removing departures who were in good academic standing from the calculation is effectively to pass them from one school's cohort to another's (assuming the student is transferring within the membership of the NCAA). Although the assumption that a student athlete who leaves a school while in good academic standing is necessarily a transfer (and, conversely, that one leaving in poor standing is not) could be debated, internal NCAA research has shown that the GSR still somewhat underestimates a true student-centered graduation rate (that is, a rate calculated by actually tracking the student from college to college until he or she earns a bachelor's degree or leaves higher education). Overall, the GSR and ASR cohort definitions significantly increase the number of student athletes who figure into rate calculations as illustrated in Table 7.2.

Each institution is required to submit the raw data needed to calculate both the federal rate and the GSR/ASR, aggregated at the level of race/ethnicity grouping within each team, to the NCAA through a password-protected Web application. The data are generally compiled and submitted by the office of institutional research or the institution's registrar's office, with assistance from personnel in the department of athletics. The input program provides separate input screens for each of five subgroups of student athletes: federal cohort, two-year transfers, four-year transfers, midyear enrollees, and nonscholarship student athletes. Within each of these five subgroups, data are broken out by seven racial/ethnic groups. Thus, institutions are requested to enter aggregated data for thirty-five categories of student athletes separately within each sport that they sponsor (although

Table 7.2. Comparison of Federal Graduation Rate and GSR Cohorts, 1998–2001 Entering Classes

	Federal Rate	GSR
Enrolled (under federal definition)	72,709	72,709
Enrolled as freshman in January	0	1,841
Two-year college transfers	0	9,085
Four-year college transfers	0	7,126
Nonscholarship athletes (only at schools not offering aid)	0	8,989
Total enrolled	72,709	99,750 (+37.2%)
Allowable exclusions (death, military, church mission)	282	354
Left eligible	0	18,655
Total denominator	72,427	80,741 (+11.5%)

NEW DIRECTIONS FOR INSTITUTIONAL RESEARCH • DOI: 10.1002/ir

some of the subgroup-by-ethnicity categories may not have any individuals included). For each of the thirty-five categories, the institution must record the number of student athletes who entered in a given academic year, the number who were "allowable exclusions" under the federal methodology (students who are to be removed from the calculation due to military service, church missions, or death), the number who left the institution in good academic standing, and the number who graduated. No personally identifiable data at the student athlete–level are submitted. In the future, these data will be extracted from the mandatory individual-level data collections in Divisions I and II (described in detail later in this chapter), eliminating the need to enter these aggregate numbers in this manner.

Once the data are collected, NCAA research consultants run a set of statistical diagnostic procedures to check for unlikely values and incomplete or missing data. When questions arise or data problems exist, the research consultants work directly with university representatives to resolve these issues. Ultimately the president or chancellor of each university must sign a form confirming that the data reported are accurate. Recently the NCAA has undertaken a limited audit program to assess the accuracy of graduation rates data reported. The primary issue identified in campus audits is a difficulty with cohort assignment of transfer students in the GSR/ASR, and educational efforts have been enhanced as a result. Once the data are finalized, the NCAA creates a specific set of public reports for each institution that meet the reporting requirements of the federal Student Right-to-Know Act (specific to the reporting of the federal graduation rate), and post those reports on the NCAA Web site. In addition, these reports are provided to all prospective student athletes as a part of the recruiting process.

Figure 7.1 presents an eighteen-year comparison of student athlete versus overall student body graduation rates using the federal methodology in Division I. Since the implementation of Proposition 48 with the entering class of 1986, the population of student athletes has consistently graduated at a slightly higher percentage than the student body at Division I schools. After 1986, the most visible increase in the national student athlete graduation rate matches the timing of a modification to the NCAA's initial academic eligibility standards in 1995 and 1996. (Commonly referred to as Proposition 16, the number of required core academic classes was increased and previous academic qualifiers with high school grades and test scores near the minimum standards were declared ineligible.) Subgroup analyses have shown in even greater detail the context of student athlete academic success. For instance, student athletes in all major race/ethnicity by gender groupings outperform their student body comparison groups by a wide margin, except for white male student athletes who graduate at a slightly lower rate than white males generally. In particular, African American female student athletes graduate at an approximately 15 percent higher rate than African American female college students, while that gap for African American males favors student athletes by approximately 10 percent. Even within

Figure 7.1. Federal Graduation Rates of All Student Athletes Versus All Students at Division I Institutions

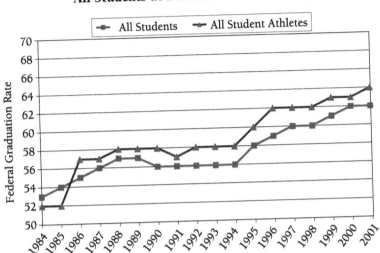

men's basketball and football, which have the lowest sport-specific graduation rates, African American males are currently graduating at a higher rate than African American males generally at those same schools.

In Figure 7.2, trends in Division I GSR are displayed for several student athlete groups over the seven cohorts that this calculation has been used. While men's basketball, football, and baseball have tended to be the lowest-performing sport groups in terms of graduation rates (either GSR or federal metric), this figure illustrates that the GSRs for those groups have had positive trends over the past several years.

Among all student athletes, the highest GSRs are seen in the women's sport groups: female student athletes across all sports show very high GSRs (roughly 90 percent on average). The sports of women's field hockey, gymnastics, lacrosse, and skiing all have GSRs of 94 percent or higher. Among men's teams, lacrosse shows the highest GSR, at 88 percent. Another important observation from the GSR data is that incoming transfers from two-year colleges graduate at lower rates than native freshmen or transfers from four-year colleges.

Data on High School Academic Performance

The adoption of Proposition 48 represented the first time that the NCAA set standards based on a core GPA as opposed to an overall high school GPA for eligibility purposes. By the early 1990s, it had become clear that institutions were defining core courses in different ways, leading to different

NEW DIRECTIONS FOR INSTITUTIONAL RESEARCH • DOI: 10.1002/ir

Figure 7.2. Seven-Year Trends in GSR for Division I Men's Basketball and Baseball and FBS Football, 1995–2001

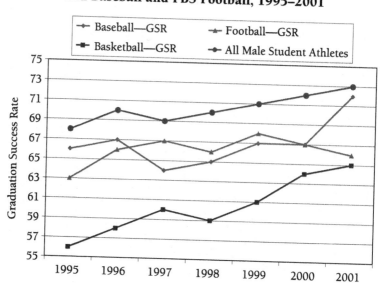

certification decisions at different schools for the same student athlete and significant fairness and competitive equity concerns. Beginning with student athletes entering Division I or II schools in 1994, the NCAA contracted with the test company ACT to create the Initial Eligibility Clearinghouse (IEC) to standardize the eligibility certification process. It was the responsibility of the IEC to determine the academic eligibility status of all prospective student athletes in these two divisions.

In the fall of 2006, eligibility certification operations were transferred to a newly created organization, the NCAA Eligibility Center (NEC), which performs essentially the same functions as did the IEC although with a greater level of automation in the data collection process. Today every high school in the country (over twenty-five thousand) is asked to send and maintain a list of courses that satisfy the NCAA's definition of core curriculum against which a student's high school transcript is compared. NCAA staff and governance committees review these core course lists to ensure that high schools are interpreting NCAA guidelines appropriately. Students are required to submit official high school transcripts to the NEC for review, along with certified ACT or SAT test score reports. Once all required data are received, computer algorithms calculate the best possible core GPA for each student athlete using the minimum required number of core courses. Because the initial academic eligibility standards are different in Divisions I and II, a separate set of algorithms is performed for each. Eligibility decisions for freshman year competition are then provided to any Division I or Division II school recruiting the student athlete.

The data collected for these processes, created to provide a fair and consistent academic certification, have proven to be phenomenally useful for conducting research for the membership of the NCAA. At the student level, data are available on all of the core curriculum courses taken by prospective student athletes, the grades in each of those courses, core curriculum and overall GPA, ACT or SAT score history, and demographic information about the students. Over 100,000 high school students annually submit data for certification purposes, with approximately 60,000 of those students completing the full certification process and eventually competing in athletics at a Division I or II member institution. In total, academic records have been compiled on almost 2 million high school students since 1994.

These data, used in combination with the individual-level academic outcomes data (to be described subsequently) to create longitudinal student records, now allow the NCAA to answer all of those questions posed about the initial-eligibility standards that could not be answered in 1986. For example, the removal of the absolute minimum test score in initial-eligibility determinations in 2003 came about based on research showing that an integrated sliding-scale of test score and GPA in core classes leads to a student athlete population that is similarly qualified academically as when the test minimums were in place, but with a higher degree of fairness at the student level. Whereas student athletes along the margin of the sliding scale standard are predicted from the data to have a similar likelihood of graduating from college, Propositions 48 and 16 declared some student athletes ineligible who had a higher likelihood of graduating than did a subset of students declared eligible. For example, a student who presented a 2.5 core GPA and an SAT score of 820 is predicted to have a roughly 38 percent chance of eventual graduation, and that student was declared eligible under Propositions 48 and 16. However, a student with a 3.0 core GPA and a test score of 700 is predicted to have a 45 percent chance of graduating but would not have been declared eligible under either of the previous initial-eligibility rules. Indeed, it was only through the analysis of these data that the impacts of the test minimum standard on racial/ethnic minority students and students from economic disadvantage were fully conveyed to the NCAA membership.

Figure 7.3 displays first-year academic outcomes for 2003 freshmen student athletes as a function of test score in SAT units (horizontal axis) and high school core course GPA (vertical axis). Student athletes in that first cohort who were newly eligible after the removal of the test minimum standard (the shaded area in the upper-left quadrant of the figure, representing students with high GPAs relative to their test scores) fared better in terms of first-year GPA, number of credits earned, and likelihood of being retained at the institution into the second year relative to a group of student athletes that has been eligible by each initial eligibility rule since 1986 (group near the middle-right part of figure with a combination of tests and grades above

Figure 7.3. First-Year Academic Performance of Division I Freshmen with Low Test Scores or Low HS GPA, 2005–2006

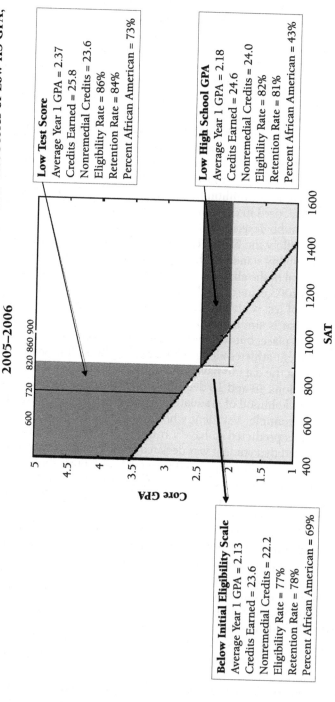

Low Test Score
Average Year 1 GPA = 2.37
Credits Earned = 25.8
Nonremedial Credits = 23.6
Eligibility Rate = 86%
Retention Rate = 84%
Percent African American = 73%

Low High School GPA
Average Year 1 GPA = 2.18
Credits Earned = 24.6
Nonremedial Credits = 24.0
Eligibility Rate = 82%
Retention Rate = 81%
Percent African American = 43%

Below Initial Eligibility Scale
Average Year 1 GPA = 2.13
Credits Earned = 23.6
Nonremedial Credits = 22.2
Eligibility Rate = 77%
Retention Rate = 78%
Percent African American = 69%

the diagonal line marking the sliding scale, but high school core GPAs between 2.0 and 2.5). Highlighting how fairness was enhanced by creating data-based standards, members of the higher-performing newly eligible group are also more likely to be from a racial/ethnic minority background than student athletes in the lower-performing comparison group.

Since 1986, the number of required core academic classes has increased gradually from eleven to sixteen. The change in this standard was based on research that indicated incremental gains in the expected graduation rate as a function of the number of core classes. That finding was supplemented by examining the core course listings provided by each high school in the country, which illustrated that almost all high schools were offering sufficient core courses to allow student athletes to meet the higher minimum thresholds. In addition, historical IEC/NEC data indicated that student athletes tended not to be adversely affected by previous core course increases, contrary to what would be seen if GPA or test score standards were raised.

Currently these data are being used by the NCAA in conjunction with the student athlete college outcomes data to develop a comprehensive risk assessment program (Facilitating Learning and Achieving Graduation) for Division I members. This program will allow colleges to compile substantial data to make informed risk assessments at the individual and aggregate levels when a student athlete enters college (to be reassessed throughout college) and match appropriate and effective (as determined through the data) support services when necessary. Clearly, having longitudinal student-level data has allowed the NCAA to take a leadership position on academic issues today that is very different from its reactive role of the 1980s and early 1990s.

Data on College Academic Performance

The data from the IEC/NEC provide significant information on the incoming characteristics of college student athletes. However, having detailed data about a student athlete's academic experiences in college linked to these high school data allows for a much more powerful analysis. Today the NCAA uses these data extensively to understand the academic trajectories of its student athletes, but reaching the point of having adequate data for this use has been arduous.

Subsequent to the implementation of Proposition 48, the NCAA set up a special committee to review and recommend academic research. That committee devised the Academic Performance Study (APS), the first large-scale academic study ever undertaken directly by the NCAA national office staff. As part of this study, Division I institutions were asked to collect outcome data on student athletes who entered their school during one of the cohorts between 1984 and 1988. This allowed for the study of two classes of student athletes who entered prior to the implementation of Proposition

48 in 1986 and three classes of student athletes who entered after the rule was in effect. A similar study was conducted in Division II around the setting of the 1988 standards. Institutions provided a set of key academic, athletic, and demographic variables, which allowed the NCAA to create a longitudinal record for each of these students that contained variables such as college GPA, annual credits earned, retention and eligibility status, and eventual graduation. Although not all institutions participated and overall sample numbers were modest in comparison to contemporary NCAA studies (several thousand longitudinal records total versus 100,000 per year now), this was a critical study for the NCAA and was used to inform many policy discussions through the mid- to late-1990s.

Beginning in 1994, the NCAA instituted a voluntary data collection in Divisions I and II: the Academic Performance Census (APC). This program was built in a similar way as the APS, except that the NCAA made an effort to collect first-year and final outcome data on every student athlete who received an athletic scholarship. Schools were also divided into cohorts as in the APS to minimize institutional burden and asked to provide yearly academic data on a single class of student athletes. The end result was a collection of several cohorts of approximately twelve thousand student athletes each, with students having varying degrees of longitudinal information provided. Over 70 percent of Division I schools participated in this voluntary effort, and these data played an important role in the development of new initial academic eligibility and progress toward degree standards that were implemented starting in 2003.

In the 2003–2004 academic year, the NCAA began requiring annual academic data reporting on all Division I scholarship student athletes (and selected nonscholarship athletes). This data collection became known as the Academic Performance Program (APP) and includes the data elements that the NCAA uses to calculate an academic progress rate (APR) for every team in Division I. This marked the first term-by-term collection of academic data on student athletes, tracking credits attempted and earned, GPAs, eligibility and retention status, and several other variables about each Division I scholarship student athlete in close to real time. Combined with the high school academic data currently collected by the NEC, the NCAA now has access to a complete longitudinal record of the academic performance from high school through college of approximately 100,000 Division I student athletes per year. Division II recently added a similar reporting requirement, and its Academic Tracking System (ATS) was up and running for the first time during the 2008–2009 academic year.

The Division I APP data and Division II ATS data are collected solely by a Web-based portal operated by the NCAA. The system is designed to interface directly with the NCAA's Compliance Assistant (CA) software (a program designed previously to assist schools with NCAA compliance issues), with other resident academic tracking systems used by member colleges, or to allow direct entry into the Web-based system. Data are collected on a student-by-student basis and then aggregated at the team level within Division I to compute a squad APR. Every Division I and II athletics program is required to submit these data annually to the NCAA as a condition of membership. Detailed information related to the collection and cleaning of the APP and ATS data (including policy guides and educational materials) is available on the Division I Committee on Academic Performance page of the NCAA Web site (http://www.ncaa.org).

The data collected in the APP are put to two major uses. The first is the calculation of the APR for every team. The APR is a real-time measure of academic performance for all the sports teams in Division I calculated by tracking the academic eligibility (as measured against NCAA eligibility standards) and retention status for every member of a team on a term-by-term basis. To calculate a team's APR, all of the retention and eligibility points that a team could have earned in a given year (points possible) are summed as the denominator, and all the points that the team actually earned (points earned) are summed as the numerator. That proportion is multiplied by 1,000 to determine the actual APR score, which is listed on a 0- to 1,000-point scale.

An example of the calculation of an APR score for a hypothetical men's football team during one academic term is shown in Table 7.3. In that term, seventy-five of the eighty-five student athletes remained academically eligible and were retained for the next term or graduated during that term, earning both an eligibility and a retention point (2 earned of 2 possible points). Three students earned 1 of 2 points because they became academically ineligible during the term, five earned 1 of 2 points because they left the college while academically eligible, and two earned 0 of 2 points due to leaving the college while academically ineligible. The APR scores reported for every

Table 7.3. APR Calculation for a Men's Football Team (N = 85 at Start of Year)

Semester 1 (Fall)	Points Earned
75 student athletes eligible and retained to next term (or graduate in that term)	75 × (2 of 2) = 150 of 150
3 student athletes are retained to next term but are academically ineligible	3 × (1 of 2) = 3 of 6
5 student athletes leave the university while academically eligible	5 × (1 of 2) = 5 of 10
2 student athletes leave the university while academically ineligible	2 × (0 of 2) = 0 of 4
Semester total	158 of 170 (929 APR)

team combine the term-by-term calculations for each of the past four years in a rolling average. The official APR scores for teams at every Division I member institution are available on the NCAA Web site.

The APR was devised in response to requests from the NCAA membership to create a measure of academic success that was strongly predictive of graduation rates. By definition, the most recent graduation rates measure a cohort of students who entered the institution a minimum of six years in the past. The APR was developed as a real-time proxy for eventual graduation rates, so that team academic success (and, potentially, academic problems) can be assessed much more rapidly than graduation rates allow. The development of the APR was possible in large measure because of the data collected in the APC study of the mid- to late-1990s; many alternative rates were generated and piloted on these data before arriving at the current formula. Although a number of complicated prediction models were proposed by various NCAA leaders, having college outcomes data from the APC study allowed us to determine that a simple equally weighted combination of eligibility and retention was as strong a predictor of graduation as any of the proposed alternatives.

Today, "APR" is one of the more recognizable acronyms in college athletics. Since the first public release of APR data in 2005 for the more than six thousand teams competing in Division I, these scores have garnered significant media attention and shed light on good and bad campus behaviors. Teams performing below particular APR cutoffs (currently 900 and 925), determined using the NCAA graduation rates and APP data sets to create APR graduation rate projections (for example, the 925 APR originally projected to a 60 percent GSR), are subject to NCAA penalties that can include public reprimand, loss of scholarships, reductions in practice time and number of contests, postseason bans, and potentially even restricted membership status. In essence, the collection of real-time college academic outcomes data enabled the discussion of student athlete academic performance to move beyond student responsibility to institutional and team accountability.

In the short time that the APP data have been compiled, the NCAA has discovered some important insights about academic performance within Division I, particularly in the sports of men's basketball, football, and baseball. For instance, in baseball it was noticed that although the student athletes begin college with better academic preparation (as measured by test scores and high school grades) than their counterparts in football and men's basketball, they tended to lose more eligibility points during their season of competition, progress more slowly toward a degree, and transfer into and out of institutions with much higher frequency than observed in other sports. As a result, certain eligibility rules were changed to incent better year-round degree progress, and transfer regulations were adopted to discourage baseball players from excessively transferring at the expense of

NEW DIRECTIONS FOR INSTITUTIONAL RESEARCH • DOI: 10.1002/ir

progress toward graduation. Early results of these research-based policy changes appear to indicate a strong positive impact on the academic behaviors among participants of the sport.

APR problems were readily apparent in men's basketball and football as well, although the data indicated that the problems manifest themselves in different ways across the two sports. Specifically, in basketball, degree attainment is hurt most not by academic failure but by retention failure. Some of these retention issues are related to professional basketball opportunities, but the majority are transfer issues, many associated with coaching changes. Football's academic problems are much more likely to be related to slow degree progress (many Division I football players are on five-year academic tracks and accumulate credits at a much slower rate than men's basketball players) and in-season academic failures.

In men's basketball, football, and baseball, the longitudinal data from the NEC and APP collections also allowed a novel look at the academic trajectories of transfer students. Statistical analyses of these data show that after controlling for academic background and various demographic variables, the act of transferring (whether from a two-year or four-year college) into Division I or between Division I schools leads to a decreased probability of graduation, especially among student athletes who are already struggling academically. As a result of these analyses, proposals are being considered on how to better prepare transfer student athletes to succeed academically in Division I.

Conclusion

The landscapes of college athletics and higher education have changed significantly since the 1980s. Media cycles are shorter, and pressure to make defensible policy decisions rapidly has arguably heightened. It was concomitant with that evolution that opportunities for the NCAA to collect student athlete academic performance data on a national scale arose. As the examples in this chapter illustrate, the use of these data in informing policy discussions among presidents, faculty, athletics directors, coaches, and student athletes during these past two decades has radically shifted the role of academics in college athletics and the role of the NCAA in higher education.

References

Adelman, C. *Answers in the Tool Box: Academic Intensity, Attendance Patterns, and Bachelor's Degree Attainment.* Washington, D.C.: U.S. Department of Education, 1999.

Adelman, C. "Making Graduation Rates Matter." *Inside Higher Ed*, Mar. 12, 2007. Retrieved Mar. 14, 2007, from http://www.insidehighered.com.

Crowley, J. N. *In the Arena: The NCAA's First Century.* Indianapolis: NCAA, 2006.

Jenkins, D. "Shift in the Use of Data Is Good News for Students." Lumina Foundation Focus, Winter 2008, 31–32. Retrieved Jan. 28, 2009, from http://www.luminafoundation.org/publications/LessonsWinter2008.pdf.

TODD A. PETR is the managing director of research at the National Collegiate Athletic Association.

THOMAS S. PASKUS is the principal research scientist at the National Collegiate Athletic Association.

8

How do sport management and higher education scholars discuss access discrimination and the underrepresentation of racial minorities in athletic administration and head coaching positions in college sport?

Decision Making in Hiring: Intercollegiate Athletics Coaches and Staff

C. Keith Harrison, Richard E. Lapchick, Neza K. Janson

. . . oh rly?

Tremendous staff, administration, and coaching opportunities are available within all levels of intercollegiate athletics. Acosta and Carpenter (2008) suggest that there has been a general increase in the number of women who hold administrative positions within the National Collegiate Athletic Association (NCAA). The study highlights 2008 as a record year for the number of women hired within intercollegiate athletics. The results demonstrated an estimated 14,742 women were employed in intercollegiate athletics with jobs ranging from athletic directors to athletic trainers (Acosta and Carpenter, 2008). There are 120 Division I Football Bowl Series schools, 116 in the Football Championship Series, and 91 nonfootball Division I institutions. Division II has 281 active member schools and Division III, 418 institutions. The National Intercollegiate Athletic Association has almost 300 member institutions, and over 500 schools are members of the National Junior College Athletic Association, the nation's largest community college athletics governing association. Among all the National Collegiate Athletic Association's 1,025 active member institutions, opportunities for employment far exceed what are available at the professional sports level.

Men, particularly white men, still overwhelmingly dominate the leadership of college athletics. Whites hold between 88 and 97 percent of all

NEW DIRECTIONS FOR INSTITUTIONAL RESEARCH, no. 144, Winter 2009 © Wiley Periodicals, Inc.
Published online in Wiley InterScience (www.interscience.wiley.com) • DOI: 10.1002/ir.316

positions in the following NCAA Division I, II, and III categories: university presidents, athletic directors, head coaches, associate athletic directors, faculty athletic representatives, and sports information directors. Whites hold 100 percent of the conference commissioner positions in Division I, excluding the historically black colleges and universities (Lapchick, 2008a).

The lack of diversity among head coaches of football teams is highly visible. Having so few African American Division I-A head football coaches continues to make headlines. At the end of the 2006 season, an African American and a Latino (Randy Shannon and Mario Cristobal) were hired as head coaches at the University of Miami (Florida) and Florida International University (FIU), respectively. In the case of FIU, it marked the first time that a school had a Latino president, athletics director, and head football coach (Lapchick, 2008a).

Finally, one of the unintended consequences of Title IX (Educational Amendments Act of 1972) has been a steep decline of women in leadership and coaching positions in women's teams. According to the Women in Intercollegiate Sports Longitudinal Study, the proportion of women in leadership of women's athletics dropped from approximately 90 percent in 1972 to 21.3 percent in 2008 (Acosta and Carpenter, 2008). Women of color are particularly rare in administration and coaching. The lack of women of color and declines for women overall have occurred despite more access to athletic opportunities for all women student athletes and the growth in the absolute number of administrative positions in intercollegiate athletics. Just over 10 percent of all athletic departments have no women administrators at all (Acosta and Carpenter, 2008).

Although the concern for fostering opportunities for women and people of color in college athletics expanded under the leadership of NCAA president Myles Brand, significant challenges in hiring decisions remain. Brand said, "Though there has been some modest recent progress, there is an intolerable lack of head football coaches who are African-American in Division I, II, and III, including especially the high-profile Division I-A level. There is an egregious lack of women and minority athletics directors and conference commissioners in all divisions. While I do not have all the answers to this frustrating problem, it is clear that we must do a better job in recruiting and selecting persons to these leadership positions" (Brand, 2003).

In terms of decision making in hiring, informal networks are a natural part of mobility patterns of individuals seeking to ascend in the coaching profession, and it creates what is known as hiring trees (Brooks, 2002), which are an intricate part of the coaching profession and have historically benefited majority (white) access versus minority (people of color) opportunities (Brooks, 2002). While some minorities and women are "players" in the majority hiring trees, the lack of women and minorities in the administration, coaching, and staffing of intercollegiate athletics is a persistent problem. Currently three main reports describe the movement of staff, coaches, and administrators in college athletics: the Racial and Gender

Report Card (Lapchick, 2008a), the Hiring Report Card (Harrison, 2008), and the Women in Intercollegiate Sport Longitudinal National Study (Acosta and Carpenter, 2008). These reports have tracked the hiring and retention of intercollegiate athletics staff, coaches, and administrators, rating the performance of specific organizations. These reports highlight the data that reflects hiring decisions in intercollegiate athletics.

Racial and Gender Report Card

The Institute for Diversity and Ethics in Sport, which is part of the College of Business Administration at the University of Central Florida (UCF) in Orlando, publishes the Racial and Gender Report Card (RGRC). Richard Lapchick has authored all reports, first at Northeastern and now at UCF (until 1998, the report was known as the Racial Report Card). Since 1989, the RGRC has tracked the hiring practices of women and people of color in intercollegiate athletics and several other leading professional, amateur, and other sporting organizations in the United States. The report considers the composition, assessed by racial and gender makeup, of student athletes, coaches, and athletic department staff and leadership in collegiate athletics departments. The institute then issues the grades in relation to overall patterns in society. Federal affirmative action policies state that the workplace should reflect the percentage of the people in the racial group in the population. Thus, with approximately 24 percent of the population being people of color, an A was achieved if 24 percent of the positions were held by people of color, B if 12 percent of the positions were held by people of color, C if it had only 9 percent, a D if it was at least 6 percent, and F for anything below that. For issues of gender, an A would be earned if 40 percent of the employees were women, B for 32 percent, C for 27 percent, D for 22 percent, and F for anything below that. The 40 percent is also taken from the federal affirmative action standard (Lapchick, 2008a).

The 2008 RGRC shows that the NCAA member institutions and their conferences lost ground for their records in gender and racial hiring practices. In fact, college sport had the lowest grade for racial hiring practices among all U.S. sporting organizations in the 2008 report (Lapchick, 2008a).

The Hiring Report Card

The Paul Robeson Research Center and the Black Coaches and Administrators (BCA) have collaborated on the Hiring Report Card for head coaches of American college football programs. Since 2003, the BCA has reported on five criteria in the hiring process of Division I football programs and assigned grades to each institution with football coaching vacancy.

At the onset of a vacancy, the athletic director and president at each of the individual institutions receive an official letter from the Paul Robeson Research Center for Academic and Athletic Prowess, informing them of the

Hiring Report Card evaluation and the five criteria. The team at the Robeson Research Center collects the data from each predominantly white institution that has a vacancy over the twelve-month period from November to October. Before the data analysis is completed, a confirmation letter is sent to each school. Each school has the opportunity to make necessary corrections to the data the researchers compiled. The signature of both the president of the university and the athletic director are required on the confirmation letter. A follow-up letter that lists the evaluation content and criteria is distributed to institutions in April and May of the following year (Harrison, 2008).

A recent trend, known as the succession trend, has started to occur in head football coaching. The trend describes the situation when a head football coach will be retiring in the near future and the successor has already been named. The BCA Task Force has determined that the grading of the institution will occur at the time the current head coach retires and the named successor assumes the head coaching position. Although a successor is named, the assignment is not final or official and may change (Harrison, 2008).

Highlights from 2003 to 2008.   The studies of the five years 2003 to 2008 show the remarkable turnover of FBS and FCS head football coaches. In the four years of the BCA HRC, there have been 148 vacancies in 217 (68 percent) schools, 92 vacancies out of 119 FBS schools graded (77 percent), and 57 vacancies out of 101 FCS schools graded (57 percent; Harrison, 2008).

The methodology used to assign grades is as follows. After the percentage of people of color in the candidate pool is determined, it is converted into a letter grade: A = 30 percent or more of people of color in the candidate pool; B = 20 to 29 percent of people of color; C = 10 to 19 percent of people of color; F = 9 percent or fewer of people of color in the candidate pool. Once the letter grade was determined, it was coded into a numerical score: A = 4, B = 5, C = 4, and F = 0 (Harrison, 2008).

On average, the schools studied in the BCA HRC, earned a "C" grade in the years 2003 to 2008. With this in mind the highest percentages of schools, regardless of division, continue to earn an A grade. However, this represents only 35 percent of the sample (fifty-one schools), which is well below half. When combined with the number of schools that earned a B final grade (forty-five schools) (30 percent), over half (ninety-six, or 64 percent) earned either an A or B. Conversely, 35 percent of the schools (fifty-two) earned less than a C grade, which is below par in terms of proactive diversity. (See the Black Coaches and Administrators Football Report Card from 2004, 2005, 2006, and 2007 [Black Coaches and Administrators, n.d.].)

Interpreting the HRC.   The major issue is how the grades from the BCA should be interpreted. On a positive note, the A grades in 2008 were the highest in five years of analyzing the head coaching vacancies. This is positive because prior to BCA HRC (2003–2004), there was no systematic process to follow or annual grades with regards to football head coaching positions (Harrison, 2008).

The purpose of grades in the HRC each year is to have an objective measurement that quantifies the five major categories used in hiring practices. Through systematic evaluation of institutions of American higher education and their athletic departments, various leaders of diversity-based organizations such as the BCA hope to increase public awareness of the limited opportunities to coaches of color based on objectivity, not subjectivity. Is the BCA HRC making a difference in terms of diversity and awareness on the topic of equitable hiring practice? Based on the data, in addition to qualifications, it appears that decision makers consider color, gender, class, family connection, and other characteristics when majority (white) or minority (people of color) are hired (Harrison, 2008).

Women in Intercollegiate Sport

The Acosta and Carpenter Study is a thirty-one-year longitudinal national study that measures the female participation and the hiring practices within intercollegiate athletics (Acosta and Carpenter, 2008). The 2008 results showed the highest female athlete participation ever, the highest number of women paid assistant coaches among women's teams, the highest number of women athletic directors, and the highest representation of women employees within intercollegiate athletics. Yet there continues to be low representation of women as coaches of women's teams; in addition, only 27.3 percent and 11.3 percent of women head athletic trainers and women head sports information directors, respectively, are female (Acosta and Carpenter, 2008).

Hiring Policies, Decision Making, and Data

The Black Coaches Association Report Card, the Racial and Gender Report Card, and the Women in Intercollegiate Sport reports continue to provide valuable data, exposing trends and patterns in college athletics hiring practices. Policies such as Title VII in the 1964 Civil Rights Act mandate equity in employment opportunities and decisions. However, further efforts are required to tackle the existing problems of exclusion in college athletics hiring practices that, despite hiring policies, remain at the forefront of these issues (Lapchick, 2008b). Data from these reports provide a systematic measure of the outcomes of hiring policies, practices, and decisions.

Title VII "made it illegal for an employer to discriminate against individuals on the basis of their race, sex, national origin, or religion, unless it is a necessary and 'bona fide occupational qualification'" (Baez, 2002, p. 13). In 1972, educational institutions were included in and covered by Title VII (Cooper, Kane, and Gisselquist, 2001). Since then, educational institutions have a duty to make certain that their hiring practices reflect the availability of women and minorities in the labor populations from which their employees are selected (Busenberg and Smith, 1997).

A critical analysis of the effects of Title VII shows that white women in higher education benefit most (Cooper, Kane, and Gisselquist, 2001). Women of color in higher education administration fare no better. According to Busenberg and Smith (1997), being a woman and a minority member is a double jeopardy for those who are seeking to have an administrative career in higher education. Although Busenberg and Smith's (1997) research was applied to presidents of universities and chief executive officers, athletic directors, athletic departments, and student athletes are also part of higher education administration and organizational culture, making minority women in athletic department leadership roles extremely rare.

Furthermore, a study conducted by Yee (2007), which focused on the interaction of race and gender and its impact on women athletics directors within the intercollegiate level, demonstrated ways of identifying strategies to ensure women of color continue their career path toward becoming head athletics directors. This is another area of research that suggests using a holistic approach to address the issues women face within intercollegiate athletics.

Another problem is that the majority of women's teams are still being coached by men. As the Coaching and Gender Equity Project suggests, the entrance for women into collegiate coaching positions has not kept pace with the dramatic changes in women's participation in collegiate athletics that was initiated by Title IX (Drago and others, 2005).

Reports such as the Hiring Report Card identify those institutions following the process and those not following it (Brand, 2003), those that are following the process and that happen to hire a person of color, and those that do not end up hiring a person of color. The empirical findings in the reports on hiring and retention in intercollegiate athletics help provide a critical examination that can inform policy and decision making. An example is seen in the 2007 initiatives and guidelines of the Division I-A (FBS) Athletic Directors Association, which were aimed at addressing the dismal record of hiring minority college football coaches. This policy, created in the spirit of the NFL's Rooney Rule, established in 2003, states that National Football League teams are required to interview minority candidates for head coaching and senior football positions. It implores colleges and universities to include minority candidates in the hiring pool for football coaching vacancies. The findings from reports should encourage some of the key stakeholders (BCA, NCAA, athletic directors, institutions, and college presidents) to work in concert to increase diversity in hiring in collegiate athletics.

Policy Recommendations and Future Research: The Diversity Progress Rate

White student athletes and white coaches should also be concerned with this issue and choose to attend or work at institutions that promote and value diversity; moreover, many of those from majority populations do care about these issues (Coakley, 1999). The following ten theoretical recommendations for discussion, extracted from the scholarly literature on management, equity, and diversity, which can be applied to sport in general in American society, will soon be applied to the Diversity Progress Rate (Harrison and Yee, 2007):

1. Raising awareness, building understanding, and encouraging reflection (see BCA Mission statement; Pless and Maak, 2004)
2. Vision of inclusion (Akers, 2006; Pless and Maak, 2004)
3. Rethought management concepts and principles (Pless and Maak, 2004; Singer, 2005)
4. Human relations management (Pless and Maak, 2004)
5. Changed power dynamics (Joplin and Daus, 1997)
6. Diversity of opinions (Goldstein, 2004; Joplin and Daus, 1997)
7. Perceived lack of empathy (Joplin and Daus, 1997)
8. Tokenism, real and perceived (Joplin and Daus, 1997)
9. Participation (Joplin and Daus, 1997)
10. Overcoming inertia or tendency to not change (Joplin and Daus, 1997)

In short, the DPR should mirror the policy patterns and cultural effects on intercollegiate athletics that the Academic Progress Rate (APR) has had. The term "APR" ignites a sense of urgency and systematic accountability and cultivates social and cultural change in the academic behaviors of all involved in college athletics. The DPR, if implemented in the same manner not only by the NCAA but, first and foremost, by member institutions, could turn the tide of diversity in terms of hiring decisions for women and minority coaches, staff, and administrators. In particular, it could be an incentive for departments to change over time. For example, departments could establish a points reward system for those who hire female and minority coaches. Finally, the institutions that receive the highest points would be those that facilitate minority employees' careers through promotion within the department or through support in accepting a higher-ranking job at another institution (as a measure of mentoring and retaining underrepresented groups).

Future research should examine the broader scope of these issues related to equity and diversity in all aspects of intercollegiate and interscholastic athletics. Investigating high schools, community colleges, and other collegiate levels such as Division II, III, and the National Intercollegiate Athletic Association can only enhance our understanding of these important decisions in college sport. Data using various theoretical models with objective and subjective measurements can inform us about the hiring and retention patterns in college sports. Although we must acknowledge that there are subjective data that are difficult to measure, institutional researchers and scholars should continue to examine hiring networks and their impact on college sports.

NEW DIRECTIONS FOR INSTITUTIONAL RESEARCH • DOI: 10.1002/ir

In 2008 alone, nearly 90 percent of major positions in college sport were held by whites, and women held 41.1 of director-level positions. In order to remedy this, "we need the stakeholders to get bold with Title VII lawsuits. We need Congress to hold hearings. We need African-American and white players alike to speak out. The system is broken when it is so exclusive. We need to fix it now" (Lapchick, 2008b, p. 34).

References

Acosta, R. V., and Carpenter, L. J. Women in Intercollegiate Sport: A Longitudinal, National Study Thirty One Year Update 1977–2008. West Brookfield, Mass.: Brooklyn College of the City University of New York, 2008.

Akers, C. R. Hiring and promoting minority professionals in college student affairs: Legal, ethical, and performance implications of practice. 2006. Unpublished paper.

Baez, B. Affirmative Action, Hate Speech, and Tenure: Narratives about Race, Law, and the Academy. New York: Routledge Falmer, 2002.

Black Coaches & Administrators. Black Coaches & Administrators Football Hiring Report Card. n.d. Retrieved from http://bcasports.cstv.com/.

Brand, M. Remarks at the BCA Hiring Report Card Symposium, Indianapolis, Ind., 2003.

Brooks, D. "African-American Coaches and Their Mobility Patterns in Sport." Paper presented at the Kinesiology Lecture Series at the University of Michigan, Ann Arbor, 2002.

Busenberg, B., and Smith, D. "Affirmative Action and Beyond: The Woman's Perspective." In M. Garcia (ed.), Affirmative Action's Testament of Hope: Strategies for a New Era in Higher Education (pp. 149–180). Albany, N.Y.: SUNY Press, 1997.

Coakley, J. "Racial differences in Sport in the 21st Century." Keynote address at the University of Michigan, Ann Arbor, Paul Robeson Research Center for Academic and Athletic Prowess Symposium #2, 1999.

Cooper, J., Kane, K., and Gisselquist, J. "Forces Eroding Affirmative Action in Higher Education: The California-Hawaii's Distinction." In B. Lindsay & M. J. Justiz (eds.), The Quest for Equity in Higher Education: Toward New Paradigms in an Evolving Affirmative Action Era (pp. 163–182). Albany: State University of New York Press, 2001.

Drago, R., and others. The Final Report for CAGE: The Coaching and Gender Equity Project. University Park: Pennsylvania State University, 2005.

Harrison, C. K. "Who You Know and Who Knows You: The Hiring Process and Practice of NCAA FBS (IA) and FCS (IAA) Head Coaching Positions." Black Coaches and Administrators Hiring Report Card 5. Paul Robeson Research Center for Academic and Athletic Prowess, the University of Central Florida, 2008.

Harrison, C. K., and Yee, S. Diversity Progress Rate (DPR). 2007. Working paper.

Goldstein, S. "Beware reverse discrimination." Law, 2004, pp. 7–8.

Joplin, J., and Daus, C. "Challenges of Leading a Diverse Workforce." Academy of Management Executive, 1997, 11(3), 32–47.

Lapchick, R. E. College Sport and NCAA. 2006–07 Racial and Gender Report Card. Orlando: Institute for Diversity and Ethics in Sport with the DeVos Sport Business Management Program in the College of Business of the University of Central Florida, 2008a.

Lapchick, R. E. "Sense of Urgency to Address Colleges' Lack of Diversity." Street and Smith's Sport Business Journal, 2008b, 11(41), 34.

Pless, N., and Maak, T. "Building an Inclusive Diversity Culture: Principles, Processes and Practice." Journal of Business Ethics, 2004, 54, 129–147.

Singer, J. "Addressing Epistemological Racism in Sport Management Research." *Journal of Sport Management*, 2005, *19*, 464–479.
Yee, S. A. "A Case Study of Career Paths for Women of Color Athletic Administrators: The Intersections of Race and Gender." Tempe: Arizona State University, 2007.

C. KEITH HARRISON *is an associate professor of the DeVos Sport Business Management Program at the University of Central Florida and the associate director of the Institute of Diversity and Ethics in Sports at the University of Central Florida.*

RICHARD E. LAPCHICK *is chair of the DeVos Sport Business Management Program at the University of Central Florida and director of both the National Consortium for Academics and Sports and the Institute for Diversity and Ethics in Sports.*

NEZA K. JANSON *is a candidate of the DeVos Sport Business Management Masters Program at the University of Central Florida.*

NEW DIRECTIONS FOR INSTITUTIONAL RESEARCH • DOI: 10.1002/ir

This chapter describes the perspectives of faculty regarding decision making and oversight of intercollegiate athletics at Division I Football Bowl Subdivision institutions and the implications for institutional researchers.

Faculty Perceptions of Intercollegiate Athletics

Janet H. Lawrence

In 1989, John S. and James L. Knight established the Knight Commission on Intercollegiate Athletics. Although it has no regulatory authority or oversight responsibilities, the Knight Commission's periodic reports are widely read and taken into account by decision-making bodies.

Beginning in 1991, the Knight Commission called for greater faculty involvement in the reform of intercollegiate athletics. These calls were joined by appeals from faculty athletics reform groups, such as the Coalition on Intercollegiate Athletics (COIA) and the Drake Group. In 2006, the Knight Commission agreed to host a national meeting, a faculty summit, with an agenda focused on ways faculty might foster and maintain balance between academics and athletics. During the planning process, it became clear that data were needed to ascertain how faculty understand the relationship between college sports and other campus activities, as well as their interest in joining reform initiatives.

This chapter provides glimpses into the development of a survey undertaken as part of the summit and offers select findings regarding faculty perceptions of how intercollegiate athletics are governed on their campuses. Recommendations for institutional research are also proposed.

Study Background

The key question before the Knight Commission was where to focus attention. Should the summit consider a range of issues—governance, finance,

New Directions for Institutional Research, no. 144, Winter 2009 © Wiley Periodicals, Inc.
Published online in Wiley InterScience (www.interscience.wiley.com) • DOI: 10.1002/ir.317

and academic—or concentrate on one aspect of intercollegiate athletics? To assist with such decisions, two advisory groups were established, one comprising representatives from different campuses and organizations concerned about the role of faculty in intercollegiate athletics (external) and another consisting of Knight Commission members and staff (internal). Intensive discussion with the external advisors resulted in an exhaustive list of issues and a heightened awareness of disparities in the perspectives of knowledgeable individuals, reflecting variations in campus contexts and personal experiences with intercollegiate athletics.

A literature review confirmed the importance of *campus setting*. For example, Cockley and Roswal (1994) and Norman (1995) find that faculty in NCAA Division II and III institutions are more satisfied with their campus athletics programs than their counterparts in NCAA Division I institutions. Noble (2004) finds that faculty on campuses with better records have more favorable attitudes toward athletics compared with faculty from schools with less successful teams.

Prior research also identified individual characteristics that may affect how faculty construct knowledge about intercollegiate athletics. Compared to their colleagues in other departments, faculty from kinesiology and physical education have more positive views of their campus's athletics programs (Harrison, 2004; Noble, 2004). Furthermore, faculty who hold governance positions and work directly with athletics are more satisfied with their institutions' athletics programs (Cockley and Roswal, 1994; Friesen, 1992).

Whether faculty members are interested in taking up the challenge of reforming intercollegiate athletics garners less attention from researchers. Trail and Chelladurai (2000), echoing the critiques of intercollegiate athletics offered by national reform groups, find that NCAA Division I faculty perceive that intercollegiate athletics is disconnected from the academic mission of their institutions. Kuga (1996) concludes that faculty in Division I universities may want to participate in athletics governance but worry about the high time commitment, as well as their competence to deal with athletics issues.

In sum, the conversations with advisory groups, combined with the mixed findings from studies of faculty that for the most part lack generalizability due to small sample sizes or single institution designs, underscored the importance of a comprehensive study. Summit discussions about faculty opinions and their potential involvement in change efforts aimed at restoring balance between intercollegiate athletics and academics needed to be informed by empirical data.

Data Collection

After meeting with the external advisors, the internal advisory group decided to focus on the most visible campuses, those within the NCAA Division I Football Bowl Subdivision (formerly Division I-A), and sample faculty with a range of intercollegiate athletic governance experiences and teaching involvement with student athletes. However, the question remained: On what content areas should attention be focused?

Interview Study.   To help with this decision, interviews were conducted with fifty-two faculty and provosts on five campuses that differed in size, location, athletic conference affiliation, and control (public versus private). After consultation with individuals on each campus and information gathered from university Web sites, interview subjects were purposively selected to include faculty engaged in institutional governance generally, and intercollegiate athletics specifically, as well as those from areas with high undergraduate enrollments who may or may not be engaged in governance beyond their departments. The semistructured interviews included questions about academic, governance, and financial issues to find out what concerns were most compelling, which areas faculty knew the most and least about, and why they would—or would not—be inclined to contribute to campus efforts to ameliorate athletics problems that most concerned them.

Another goal of the interviews was to find ways to capture the attention of faculty who indicate minimal interest and engagement with matters pertaining to college sports. Documents available from COIA, the American Association of University Professors, and the Drake Group offer insights into what is on the minds of faculty invested in the reform of intercollegiate athletics. However, given that a goal of the summit was to build faculty support, we paid particular attention to what those who professed little knowledge had to say and how they articulated their concerns. This proved to be critical as we framed survey questions.

Survey Instrument Development.   The interviews resulted in four key decisions. First, faculty interest appeared to be evenly distributed across academic, finance, and governance matters. Thus, data relevant to all three would be collected. Second, faculty perceptions of intercollegiate athletics intertwine with their views of the larger campus context. Consistent with prior research such as that by Cockley and Roswal (1994), professors' beliefs about athletics are shaped by their experiences in various domains of campus life. For example, their experiences with admissions for performance majors or family legacies influence their beliefs about special admissions of student athletes; levels of departmental resources affect how they respond to the financing of college sports; and perceptions of campus values regarding shared governance in general influence their views of faculty oversight of intercollegiate athletics. Therefore, we included parallel survey questions about campus policies and practices related and unrelated to athletics. For instance, one set of items inquired about academic advising of all undergraduate students, and another set asked about academic advising for student athletes.

The third decision was to assess respondents' prioritization of intercollegiate athletics in relation to other campus issues pressing for faculty attention, including student financial aid or resources for research. And finally, given research on faculty work-related decisions (Blackburn and Lawrence, 1995) and interview findings, we chose to assess intentions to become involved in campus reform initiatives in areas where personal investment is likely to be strong. Questions about joining campus change efforts focus on the specific athletics-related concern each respondent cited as personally most important.

The faculty survey questionnaire contains both open-ended and Likert-type items distributed across five sections:

- *Perceptions and Beliefs* (Likert-type questions): Faculty indicate on a scale ranging from Not at All to Very Much (and including Don't Know and Not Relevant options) the extent to which they believe selected institutional policies and practices, as well as behaviors and attitudes of students, student athletes, campus administrators, coaches, and faculty, apply to their campuses.
- *Satisfaction* (Likert-type questions): Respondents indicate on a scale ranging from Very Dissatisfied to Very Satisfied (including a Not Relevant option as well) their satisfaction with general and athletics-specific policies, practices, and conditions on their campuses (such as the use of special admissions for high school athletes who do not meet regular academic standards) as well as student, administrator, and faculty behavior related to governance, academics, and finance (including that athletes are good representatives of the university in their public behavior and statements to the press).
- *Campus Priorities:* Individuals indicate on a scale of Very Low to Very High the priority they believed faculty governance groups must give over the next five years to each of thirteen areas confronting faculty governance bodies, including intercollegiate athletics.
- *Major Concerns:* An open-ended item asks faculty what most concerns them about intercollegiate athletics on their campus. Respondents who state a concern are asked to indicate the chances they would join a campus-based initiative to address this problem and estimate the likelihood that such an activity would result in meaningful change on their campus.
- *Demographic Characteristics:* Questions address the respondents' careers (for example, tenure status, field of teaching, years at institution) as well as their experience with faculty governance, intercollegiate athletics and student athletes, their sources of information about intercollegiate athletics, their current investment of time in undergraduate teaching, research and service, and their personal experiences as student-athletes.

The Faculty Survey (see Lawrence, Hendricks, and Ott, 2007, for a copy of instrument) was made available to respondents both online and in paper format. The online version was programmed so that a participant could exit and resume the survey at any time with previously completed responses already saved on the screen. On average, the questionnaire required twenty to thirty minutes to complete.

Sampling Strategy. Given that one goal was to paint a comprehensive picture of faculty beliefs about intercollegiate athletics, a purposive sample was drawn from the population of 119 Division I Football Bowl Subdivision (FBS) institutions classified by the NCAA in 2006. To ensure geographical coverage, two universities were randomly selected from each of the eleven FBS conferences, and one was randomly drawn from the unaffiliated campuses. We then used online information and campus directories to choose tenure-track faculty on each campus who were currently involved in institution-level campus governance (such as faculty senates) or in roles associated with the oversight of intercollegiate athletics (for example, Faculty Athletic Representatives, members of campus athletics advisory boards, or NCAA certification teams) and who had appointments in fields that typically enroll larger numbers of undergraduate students, thus increasing the chances of interactions between respondents and student athletes. We assumed the latter group includes individuals whose involvement in the oversight of intercollegiate athletics differs. However, the sample was limited to tenure-track faculty because on some campuses, governance committee membership may be limited to this group.

E-mail messages were sent to 14,187 faculty members on twenty-three campuses. Out of this group, 13,604 individuals received invitations to participate, and 3,005 completed the survey, for an overall response rate of 23 percent, a rate typical for online surveys (Sheehan, 2001). Although the response was low, nevertheless it was encouraging given that we sought participation from people we knew had scant interest in the focal topic. Adjusted for those who did not fully complete the survey, faculty on sabbatical, emeritus faculty, non-tenure-track faculty, and administrators inadvertently included, the final individual sample used in the analyses was 2,071.

The selection strategy produced a sample that resembles the national profile of faculty in its distribution across gender, race, professorial ranks, and tenure status. Three campuses are private, and twenty are public. More than 75 percent of survey respondents currently teach or have in the past taught student athletes, and 14 percent say they are now serving, or in the past have served, in intercollegiate athletics governance roles (see Lawrence, Hendricks, and Ott, 2007).

Data Analysis and Results

After reviewing the preliminary findings, the internal advisory committee decided a digest of primarily descriptive statistics would best serve to frame summit topics and ground discussions across the range of topics. However, subsequent analyses have been undertaken to assess faculty support for different reform proposals (Lawrence, Ott, and Hendricks, 2007), respond to a historical analysis of faculty oversight (Lawrence, 2008), and explore theoretical propositions about faculty perceptions and prioritization of intercollegiate athletics as a governance issue (Lawrence and Ott, 2008). Findings from these studies that shed light on faculty perspectives regarding campus

NEW DIRECTIONS FOR INSTITUTIONAL RESEARCH • DOI: 10.1002/ir

decision making and oversight of college sports—and their interest in inter-collegiate athletics as a governance area—are presented next.

Faculty Perceptions of Decision Making. Descriptive analyses of total sample responses indicate that faculty feel disconnected from intercollegiate athletics decision making. Although the American Association of University Professors (1989) and COIA (2004) specify athletics as an area for shared decision making by faculty and administrators, the majority (62 percent) believes intercollegiate athletics is an auxiliary enterprise that is structurally separate and accountable to administrators, not faculty. Furthermore, most (40 percent) perceive that faculty roles associated with overseeing college sports on their campuses are ill defined, and more than a third (35 percent) believe administrators are not forthcoming with information that governance committees need to ensure the quality of student athletes' educational experiences.

Given such findings, it is not surprising that faculty tend to be displeased with their intercollegiate athletics governance roles: 42 percent are dissatisfied with the extent to which faculty input informs administrative decisions, and 44 percent are dissatisfied with the range of faculty perspectives considered by central administrators who formulate institutional positions on intercollegiate athletics. Faculty members are also skeptical about the influence of off-campus groups. Half say that decisions about intercollegiate athletics on their campuses are driven by the priorities of an entertainment industry that is not invested in their university's academic mission, and 40 percent think athletics boosters who put winning sports records ahead of academic standards have influence with their presidents. Yet more of the faculty who express an opinion (46 percent) are satisfied than are dissatisfied (28 percent) with presidential oversight, and more are satisfied (42 percent) than are dissatisfied (34 percent) with institutional control of intercollegiate athletics. This outcome reflects the fact that faculty involved in athletics governance are less likely to say they have no opinion and are more likely to hold positive views.

Juxtaposing faculty perceptions of how administrators engage them in various institutional-level decisions reveals instances where they think athletics is treated differently. The majority (54 percent) believe faculty governance groups advise campus administrators on academic matters, while 48 percent believe it is not common practice for faculty governance groups to advise administrators on intercollegiate athletics decisions. Many respondents think it is not common practice for administrators to consult with faculty governance groups on budgeting for either the athletics department (49 percent) or academic units (49 percent).

These results portray the predominant views within the total sample. However, consistent with previous studies, we found that individual perspectives vary in relation to personal experiences and campus contexts, and any composite may mask deviations among faculty groups. Respondents with the most experience in athletics oversight are most satisfied with governance, and those with no experience are least satisfied. As noted earlier, those more experienced are satisfied with presidential oversight and institutional control over intercollegiate athletics and the level of cooperation between the athletics department and faculty groups responsible for upholding academic standards. The least experienced faculty are dissatisfied with all aspects of governance, and particularly the range of faculty perspectives considered by central administrators when institutional positions on intercollegiate athletics are formulated.

The results of regression analyses provide supplementary evidence that faculty beliefs about intercollegiate athletics are shaped by their experiences in other domains of college life. To illustrate, faculty who strongly believe academic issues are resolved at their university through collaborative decision making with administrators are significantly more likely to believe faculty are involved in decisions about intercollegiate athletics. Faculty members who are the most skeptical about collaborative decision making are significantly more likely to perceive the athletics department as an auxiliary enterprise with ambiguous policies and practices.

To further examine the impact of campus context, we created a taxonomy that differentiates sampled institutions along two dimensions: academics and athletics performance. With the advice of internal project advisors, variables representing each dimension were identified and, for each institution, combined into composite measures representing overall athletics performance and overall academic performance. Due to the relatively small number of institutions sampled, the continua were divided in half at the median calculated score for the overall sample. The result is a two-by-two taxonomy, distinguishing among institutions above and below the average in one or both of academic and athletics performance (see Lawrence, Hendricks, and Ott, 2007, for details).

Qualitative analyses of all faculty responses within each of the quadrants were completed, and predominant patterns in their perceptions and concerns were abstracted. We found that faculty from the Lower Academic Performance/Lower Athletic Performance and the Lower Academic Performance/Higher Athletic Performance institutions expressed apprehensions about oversight, albeit different ones. Those in the former group are dissatisfied with athletics governance and the perceived subsidization of college sports at the expense of academics. They want to give higher priority to intercollegiate athletics as a faculty governance issue. Faculty members in the latter group are troubled by the structural separation and power of athletics departments combined with the apparent influence of external groups on intercollegiate athletics decisions.

Faculty Indifference. Within the total sample, the largest group of respondents (47 percent) perceives their colleagues are interested in athletics governance issues. Yet when asked to prioritize a list of thirteen issues confronting faculty governance bodies today, intercollegiate athletics places next to last in terms of importance.

Furthermore, more than a third of the faculty say they lack sufficient knowledge or have no opinion about issues central to the efforts of reform groups and matters pertaining to campus oversight of intercollegiate athletics—for example, the types of intercollegiate athletics governance roles that faculty assume and the levels of cooperation between athletics and academic departments at their universities. Given such data, it is tempting to conclude faculty do not know and do not care; they are indifferent. However, this is like saying that people who do not know the Dow Jones closing average do not care about the economy. This is an overgeneralization.

We explored the complex empirical links between knowledge and caring by first creating variables to represent each respondent's level of knowledge about intercollegiate athletics governance (the percentage of "don't know" responses) and several indexes of "caring": (1) the personal priority they give to intercollegiate athletics as a campus governance matter, (2) the self-reported likelihood they would join a campus initiative to address their personal concerns, and (3) their subjective estimates of the probability that faculty initiatives designed to improve intercollegiate athletics would result in meaningful change on their campus. Analyses were conducted to determine if less informed faculty were more likely to be indifferent.

We found that a lack of knowledge about governance significantly decreases the odds that faculty members would join a campus change initiative but does not affect their sense that efforts would lead to change. When the level of knowledge and potential impact data are graphed, the two lines are essentially parallel, suggesting that those who are pessimistic about the impact of athletics-related campus initiatives are cynical no matter how much knowledge they possess (Lawrence, 2008).

Another set of analyses was undertaken to find out if faculty perceptions of organizational politics (POP) around intercollegiate athletics decisions affect their prioritization of intercollegiate athletics as a governance matter. Two indicators of POP, *speaking out* (in other words, individuals are discouraged from being critical of administrators) and *in-groups* (cliques with power that hinder organizational effectiveness) were analyzed (Lawrence and Ott, 2008).

Several findings are germane to this discussion. First, the more that faculty members know about governance matters, the less they perceive that athletics in-groups (such as boosters, the media, politicians) are able to exert strong power over decision making, even after controlling for involvement in intercollegiate athletics governance. Second, the more that faculty members believe in-groups are able to exert power and influence over campus decisions, the less satisfied they are with faculty governance involvement in decisions about intercollegiate athletics. Third, the more that faculty members perceive their representatives are silenced from having a voice in athletics decisions, the less satisfied they are with overall faculty input to such decisions. Fourth, respondents who believe they are allowed to voice their views on intercollegiate athletics assign higher priority to athletics as a governance issue.

Conclusions and Implications for Future Research

Given the need for baseline information across a range of issues, the faculty survey is comprehensive. A trade-off was made between breadth and depth of topic coverage. Although intercollegiate athletics issues are interrelated, in-depth pursuit of one area (in this case, campus oversight of varsity sports) would have produced more nuanced knowledge about faculty views. For instance, we would have liked to know what problems faculty associate with intercollegiate athletics on their campuses, what governance groups faculty think are designated responsibility for resolving each of these issues, and what priority they would assign to each problem. Such information could help guide local efforts to enhance oversight policies and practices.

When gathering and interpreting data, researchers need to systematically consider the contextualized nature of faculty perceptions of intercollegiate athletics. Within NCAA divisions, there are myriad institutional characteristics that have not been systematically examined and need to be considered. At the broadest level, our interviews and preliminary analyses of survey data suggest that regional differences—for example, the presence of a professional sports team—can affect faculty beliefs. At the campus level, a number of contextual factors, such as the general governance climate and financial well-being of a university, affect faculty views.

Nevertheless, creating institution-level variables presents methodological challenges. When we created our institutional taxonomy, we found we could not reconcile data from relevant reports because institutional decisions regarding the categorization of expenses were neither transparent nor consistent (for example, several choices about how to report athletics financial data to the Integrated Postsecondary Education Data System and in accordance with the Equity in Athletics Disclosure Act are left to the discretion of institutions). In addition, variations in benchmarks and statistics used to represent athletic and academic performance differed, and choosing between them altered the classification of campuses. We originally used the NCAA four-class graduation rate statistic as one of the grouping criteria. When the decision was made to replace this statistic with the six-class graduation rate, three schools moved from one institutional taxonomy category to another due to major differences in their performance on these two measures.

The faculty survey provides partial answers and a foundation for future inquiries into why faculty knowledge and interest in the governance of intercollegiate athletics may fluctuate. The dearth of research in this area, combined with calls for greater faculty involvement in national reforms, intensifies the need for inquiries beyond the single campus case studies that predominate.

References

American Association of University Professors. "The Role of the Faculty in the Governance of College Athletics." 1989. Retrieved on Jan. 27, 2008, from http://www.aaup.org/AAUP/comm/rep/athgov.htm.

Blackburn, R., and Lawrence, J. *Faculty at Work*. Baltimore: Johns Hopkins University Press, 1995.

Coalition on Intercollegiate Athletics (COIA). "Campus Athletics Governance, the Faculty Role: Principles, Proposed Rules, and Guidelines." 2004. Retrieved Jan. 27, 2008, from http://www.neuro.uoregon.edu/~tublitz/COIA/Governance.html.

Cockley, W., and Roswal, G. "A Comparison Study of Faculty Members' Perceived Knowledge and Satisfaction Regarding NCAA Athletic Programs." *Journal of Sport Behavior*, 1994, 17(4), 217–223.

Friesen, R. "A Comparison of NCAA Division 1-A Coaches' and Administrators' Attitudes Toward Issues in Intercollegiate Athletics." Unpublished doctoral dissertation, University of Kansas, 1992.

Harrison, T. "Internal Stakeholder Perceptions of Intercollegiate Athletic Reform: A Focus Group Examination." Unpublished doctoral dissertation, Ohio State University, 2004.

Kuga, D. "Governance of Intercollegiate Athletics: Perceptions of Faculty Members." *Journal of Sport Management*, 1996, 10, 149–168.

Lawrence, J. "Academics and Athletics: Do Position and Field of Play Matter?" *Journal of Intercollegiate Sport*, 2008, 1(1), 84–97.

Lawrence, J., Hendricks, L., and Ott, M. "Faculty Survey: Knight Commission National Study of Faculty Perceptions of Intercollegiate Athletics." 2007. Retrieved Jan. 27, 2008, from http://www.knightcommission.org/about/faculty_perceptions_of_intercollegiate_athletics_survey/.

Lawrence, J., and Ott, M. "Organizational Politics and Faculty Governance Priorities." Paper presented at the Annual Meeting of the Association for the Study of Higher Education, Jacksonville, Fla., Nov. 2008.

Lawrence, J., Ott, M., and Hendricks, L. "Faculty and the Reform of Intercollegiate Athletics: A Study of Faculty Oversight of Intercollegiate Athletics and Implications for National Policy Initiatives." Paper presented at the Annual Meeting of the Association for the Study of Higher Education, Louisville, Ky., Nov. 2007.

Noble, J. "Faculty Attitudes Toward NCAA Division III Athletic Programs." Unpublished doctoral dissertation, University of Northern Colorado, 2004.

Norman, G. "Faculty Attitudes Toward Intercollegiate Athletics at Colleges and Universities Belonging to Division I of the National Collegiate Athletic Association and the National Association of Intercollegiate Athletics." Unpublished doctoral dissertation, University of North Texas, 1995.

Sheehan, K. "E-mail Survey Response Rates: A Review." *Journal of Computer Mediated Communication*, 2001, 6(2). Retrieved June 18, 2007, from http://jcmc.indiana.edu/vol6/issue2/sheehan.html.

Trail, G., and Chelladurai, P. "Perceptions of Goals and Processes of Intercollegiate Athletics: A Case Study." *Journal of Sport Management*, 2000, 14, 154–178.

JANET H. LAWRENCE *is Associate Professor at the Center for the Study of Higher and Postsecondary Education, School of Education, University of Michigan. Special acknowledgment goes to Molly Ott, graduate research assistant at the Center for the Study of Higher and Postsecondary Education, for her contributions to this chapter.*

10

URLs to a wide range of resources on athletics data and a glossary of terms are provided.

Selected Resources and Glossary

Daisy D. Alfaro, Jennifer Lee Hoffman

Intercollegiate athletics is no longer an area of interest solely for coaches and athletic administrators; increasingly, this field has captured the curiosity of faculty, researchers, and the general public. Such attention has the potential to greatly affect the course the field of intercollegiate athletics takes in the years to come. Conveniently, access to information and data on intercollegiate athletics has become readily and widely available. This chapter serves as an introduction to the numerous resources and terms related to intercollegiate athletics data. Most of the resources related to data-driven decision making in intercollegiate athletics described in this volume are available online at http://depts.washington.edu/nidr2009.

Selected Resources

Academic progress rate (APR). Provides summary APR data as well as APR data by school. http://www.ncaa.org/wps/ncaa?ContentID=276.

American Association of University Professors (AAUP). Provides access to publications and research reports on intercollegiate athletics and higher education. http://www.aaup.org/aaup.

American College of Sports Medicine (ACSM). A sports medicine and exercise science organization leading in the science of exercise; diagnosis, treatment, and prevention of sport-related injuries. The site also provides funding resources for researchers interested in sports medicine. www.acsm.org.

CAGE: The Coaching and Gender Equity Project. A report that explores issues contributing to the underrepresentation of women in coaching positions of women's collegiate teams. Provides recommendations to ensure gender equity in collegiate athletics. http://lser.la.psu.edu/workfam/cage.htm.

NEW DIRECTIONS FOR INSTITUTIONAL RESEARCH, no. 144, Winter 2009 © Wiley Periodicals, Inc.
Published online in Wiley InterScience (www.interscience.wiley.com) • DOI: 10.1002/ir.318

Coalition on Intercollegiate Athletics (COIA). The Division I-A Faculty Senate Coalition provides policy papers and reports on intercollegiate athletics and higher education. http://www.neuro.uoregon.edu/~tublitz/COIA/.

College Sports Project (CSP). Invites colleges and universities sponsoring Division III athletics interested in strengthening the bonds between intercollegiate athletics and educational values to participate in ongoing research and integration efforts. http://www.collegesportsproject.org.

Datalys Center for Sports Injury Research and Prevention. National nonprofit that helps researchers conduct injury surveillance and research projects that translate information into better prevention, public health, and sports medicine outcomes. http://www.datalyscenter.org/.

Division I Athletics Certification Program. Established by the NCAA to ensure transparency and compliance to the principles of intercollegiate athletics. http://www.ncaa.org/wps/ncaa?ContentID=37341.

Drake Group. A national network of college faculty interested in reform of intercollegiate athletics. Publications and research reports on intercollegiate athletics and higher education are available. http://www.thedrakegroup.org.

Equity in Athletics Data Analysis Cutting Tool. U.S. Department of Education's Office of Postsecondary Education searchable database. Provides customized reports on one institution as well as aggregated data for a group of colleges and or universities. http://ope.ed.gov/athletics/.

Government Accountability Office. Provides accountability reports to the U.S. Congress on topics related to intercollegiate athletics. http://www.gao.gov/.

Higher Education Research Institute (HERI). Administers several surveys on attitudes, values, and experiences of college students. Also administers the Cooperative Institutional Research Program Freshman Survey, a longitudinal study surveying first-year students at over nineteen hundred institutions, and houses the College Students' Beliefs and Values survey administered by the Spirituality in Higher Education Project. Housed at the University of California, Los Angeles. http://www.gseis.ucla.edu/heri/index.php.

Institute for Diversity and Ethics in Sport. Provides reports of student athlete graduation rates, racial attitudes in sports, and hiring practices in coaching and athletic administration. http://www.tidesport.org/.

Knight Commission on Intercollegiate Athletics. Formed by university presidents and trustees, faculty, and former student athletes to propose reform efforts that emphasize academic values in an arena where commercialization of college sports often overshadows the underlying goals of higher education. This site makes available publications and research reports on this topic. http://www.knightcommission.org/.

National Center for Catastrophic Sport Injury Research. Publishes three reports annually that highlight data on fatal and catastrophic injuries pertaining to the brain or spinal cord. http://www.unc.edu/depts/nccsi/.

National Collegiate Athletic Association (NCAA). Provides data and reports on the academic performance and educational experience of student athletes among member institutions. www.ncaa.org.

National Federation of State High School Associations (NFHS). Administers the Participation Figures Search survey that provides the number of high schools offering a specific sport. Also provides a history of boys' and girls' high school participation rates in particular sports. www.nfhs.org.

National Survey of Student Engagement (NSSE). A survey that assesses undergraduate educational experiences, particularly concerning how students spend their time and what they gain from the college experience. http://www.nsse.iub.edu/index.cfm.

NCAA Diversity and Inclusion Resources. A list of resources providing historical information, clarifications, policy information, and professional development that can inform diversity and inclusion efforts. http://www.ncaa.org/wps/ncaa?ContentID=1322.

New Directions for Institutional Research • DOI: 10.1002/ir

NCAA Gender Equity Resources. Provides information on programs, publications, and resources related to gender equity. http://www.ncaa.org/wps/ncaa?ContentID=286.

NCAA Injury Surveillance System (ISS). A resource that provides injury and exposure data for evidence-based decision making on health and safety issues. http://www.ncaa.org/wps/ncaa?ContentID=1126.

NCAA Sports Sponsorship and Participation Rates Report. Presents statistical data on average squad sizes by gender, division, and sport. http://www.ncaapublications.com/ProductsDetailView.aspx?sku=PR2009&AspxAutoDetectCookieSupport=1.

U.S. Department of Education, Office of Civil Rights. Provides assistance to institutions to address and prevent discrimination and comply with civil rights laws. http://www.ed.gov/about/offices/list/ocr/index.html.

U.S. Department of Education, Office of Postsecondary Education. Provides access to information on programs, policy initiatives, reports, and resources on issues of access and quality of postsecondary education. http://www.ed.gov/about/offices/list/ope/index.html.

Women in Intercollegiate Sport: A Longitudinal, National Study. Since 1977 has reported on the status of women coaches, staff, and administrators at NCAA member institutions. http://webpages.charter.net/womeninsport/.

Women's Sports Foundation Research and Policy Institute. Issues publications, research reports, essays, position papers, and policy statements on gender and athletics. http://www.womenssportsfoundation.org/.

Glossary

Academic Performance Census (APC). Beginning in 1994, the NCAA instituted the APC as a voluntary data collection built in a similar way as the Academic Performance Study (APS) for all Division I and II programs. Longitudinal data that tracks first-year academic performance and final outcome data on every student athlete who received an athletic scholarship. In 2009, Division II began requiring APC data from all its institutions.

Academic Performance Program (APP). In the 2003–2004 academic year, the NCAA began requiring annual academic data reporting on all Division I scholarship student athletes (and selected non-scholarship athletes). This includes the data elements that the NCAA uses to calculate an academic progress rate for every Division I team. *See* Academic progress rate.

Academic progress rate (APR). Tracks progress to degree using credits attempted and earned, grade point averages, and eligibility and retention status for every Division I scholarship student athlete. Division I colleges that do not offer athletics-related financial aid are exempt from reporting the federal rate (primarily Ivy League schools and military academies).

Academic success rate (ASR). Tracks progress to graduation at Division II institutions. Includes students not receiving athletics aid, in recognition of the high percentage of Division II student athletes who fall into this category.

Acclamation period. A five-day progression at the start of preseason practice that allows student athletes to acclimate to exercise intensity, the addition of equipment in the heat, and environmental stressors. Includes provisions for days with multiple practice sessions.

American Medical Society for Sports Medicine (AMSSM). An organization of physicians committed to the advancement of research and practice in the field of sports medicine.

American Society for Testing of Materials International (ASTM). An international organization addressing the standardization needs in numerous industries.

Committee on Competitive Safeguards and Medical Aspects of Sports (CSMAS). Provides research and leadership development opportunities that promote a healthy and safe environment for student athletes. *See* National Injury Surveillance System (ISS).

Convenience sample. The selection of a population on the basis of accessibility or the researcher's discretion.

Division I-A, I-AA, I-AAA. Former categorization of institutions with football teams. Division I-AAA, however, classified schools that did not have a football team. *See* Football Bowl Subdivision; Football Championship Series.

Duplicated count. Counts an athlete once for each sport in which he or she participates. Used for determining sport participation opportunities.

Emerging sports. NCAA designation that gives certain sports seeking to achieve gender equity greater visibility and support. If a sport gains enough teams, it moves from emerging to championship sport status.

Equity in Athletics Disclosure Act (EADA). Mandates requiring colleges to report the number of students on each men's and women's athletic teams; the amount of money spent on athletic scholarships for male and female students; the numbers of male and female coaches for men's and women's teams; and the total revenues and expenses from the institution's intercollegiate athletic activities.

Equivalency sport. NCAA term for determining the limit on the number of scholarships that may be offered per sport. The school may divide up a single scholarship among more than one athlete. Examples of equivalency sports (and the number of scholarships that may be offered) are field hockey (twelve), golf (six), lacrosse (twelve), rowing (twenty), soccer (fourteen), softball (twelve), track and field/cross country (eighteen), and swimming/diving (fourteen). *See also* Head count sport.

Evidence-based decision making. The process of relying on experts, research, and knowledge of a field to formulate informed decisions or recommendations.

Football Bowl Subdivision (FBS). Category of Division I football garnering the most visibility; eligible for participation in bowl games sponsored by the Bowl Championship Series. Formerly Division I-A.

Football Championship Series (FCS). Category of Division I football programs that do not participate in the Bowl Championship Series. Formerly Division I-AA.

Graduation rates (federal). Term that indicates the percentage of undergraduates completing a degree program.

Graduation success rate (GSR). Tracks progress to degree completion in Division I institutions. The GSR takes into account transfer students and allows for students who leave institutions prior to graduation be subtracted from graduation rate calculation. *See also* Academic success rate.

Head count sport. NCAA term for determining the limit on the number of scholarships that may be offered per sport. No more than the designated number of individuals (head counts) may receive aid (such as twelve head count for gymnastics, twelve for women's volleyball, and eight for women's tennis). *See also* Equivalency sport.

Initial Eligibility Clearinghouse (IEC). Since 1994 has determined the academic eligibility status of all prospective student athletes entering Division I and II schools. *See* National Eligibility Center.

National Association of Intercollegiate Athletics (NAIA). A governing organization with approximately 300 member institutions that promotes student athlete academic achievement, character development, and athletic success.

National Athletic Trainers' Association (NATA). An organization that provides support and advocacy on behalf of those in the athletic training profession.

National Eligibility Center (NEC). Determines the academic eligibility status of all prospective student athletes entering Division I and II schools since autumn 2006. *See* Initial Eligibility Clearinghouse.

National Injury Surveillance System (ISS). Monitors injury trends to enhance safety in intercollegiate athletics. Injury and exposure data are collected yearly from a volunteer sample of NCAA member institutions. The goal of the NCAA injury surveillance program is to monitor and reduce injury rates through suggested changes in rules, protective equipment, medical care policy, or coaching techniques. See Committee on Competitive Safeguards and Medical Aspects of Sports.

Office of Civil Rights (OCR). The U.S. Department of Education agency responsible for oversight and enforcement of Title IX.

Proposition 48. The first NCAA initial academic eligibility standards based on a core grade point average (GPA). Prior to Proposition 48, overall high school GPA was used for freshmen eligibility purposes.

Random sample. Selection of a population through a random but controlled selection where each individual has the same probability of being chosen.

Regression analysis. Implements a linear model to data to predict the values of the dependent variable from a number of independent variables.

Risk management decision making. The process of relying on assessment of risks to make an informed decision. For example, recommendations for assignment of athletic trainers to activities are based on risk and comparison of institutional injury rates with divisional and national totals.

Student Right-to-Know Act. Mandated the reporting of student athlete graduation rates, financial assistance awarded, and crime statistics for institutions receiving federal Title IV funding.

Substantially proportionate. One of three options for determining compliance with the participation provision of Title IX. Based on overall undergraduate enrollment. Also known as *proportionality* and *prong 1. See also* Three-part test.

Three-part test. Used to determine if a college is providing equitable sport participation opportunities. To comply with prong 1 (proportionality), the percentage of male and female student athletes should reflect the student body. To comply with prong 2, the college must have a history and continuing practice of program expansion for the underrepresented. To comply with prong 3, a college must accommodate the interests and abilities of the underrepresented gender. A college must meet only one of the three prongs in order to be considered in compliance with Title IX's equitable sport participation opportunity provision.

Title IV. Federal law passed in 1965 as part of the Higher Education Act, providing financial assistance for students by increasing federal aid to higher education institutions and students.

Title VII. Federal law passed in 1964 as part of the Civil Rights Act, mandating equity in employment opportunities and decisions. Educational institutions were included under Title VII in 1972.

Title IX. Federal law passed in 1972 as part of the Education Amendments of 1972. Changed to the Patsy T. Mink Equal Opportunity in Education Act in 2002 to honor the primary author. Known widely for its implications in education-based sport programs, Title IX requires equity in ten key areas of education: access, career education, employment, math and science, standardized testing, athletics, education for pregnant and parenting students, learning environment, sexual harassment, and technology.

Unduplicated count. Counts an athlete as one regardless of whether the individual participates in more than one sport. Used for determining scholarship ratios.

DAISY D. ALFARO *is a doctoral student in the Educational Leadership and Policy Studies Program and research assistant in the Center for Leadership in Athletics at the University of Washington.*

JENNIFER LEE HOFFMAN *is a research associate with the Center for Leadership in Athletics at the University of Washington.*

INDEX

Academic classes, 87
Academic performance, data collection, 78
Academic Performance Census (APC), 88, 90
Academic Performance Program (APP), 88–91
Academic Performance Study (APS), 87, 88
Academic Progress Rate (APR), 88–91, 99
Academic Success Rate (ASR), 80–81, 82
Academic Tracking System (ATS), 88, 89
Academic year, 56
ACE (American Council on Education), 23
Acosta, R. V., 93, 94, 95, 97
ACT scores, 77, 84
Add-on (incremental) budgeting, 13–14
Adelman, C., 79, 80
AIR (Association for Institutional Research), 37
Akers, C. R., 99
American Association of University Professors, 105, 108
American College Athletics, 21
American Council on Education (ACE), 23
American Football Coaches Association, 59, 61
Andrew W. Mellon Foundation, 66
APC (Academic Performance Census), 88, 90
APP (Academic Performance Program), 88–91
APR (Academic Progress Rate), 88–91, 99
APS (Academic Performance Study), 87, 88
Arenas/stadiums, 19, 22, 27
Aries, D., 66, 69, 73
Aries, E., 35
Arms race metaphor, 27–28
Asch, M., 67
Association for Institutional Research (AIR), 37
ASR (Academic Success Rate), 80–81, 82
ATS (Academic Tracking System), 88, 89
Astin, A. W., 34
Athlete exposure (A-E), 55; exposure form collection, 57

Athletes: expectations of current, 33–34; learning and development of, 36–39; undergraduate experience of, 34–36
Athletic departments, 19–25, 28–29
Athletic Directors Association, 98
Athletics Disclosure Act, 47–48
Athletics programs, as independent functions, 21–22
Athletics regulations under Title IX, 44
Attitude improvement, 16
Atwell, R. H., 24, 26

Bachelor's degrees, 79
Baez, B., 97
Balloou, J., 67
Baseball, 59
Basic Academic Skills Survey (BASS), 37
Basketball, 48
BASS (Basic Academic Skills Survey), 37
BCA (Black Coaches and Administrators), 95–96, 97
Beliefs, faculty, 106
Bentley, H. W., 21, 22
Bergeron, M. F., 60
Berkowitz, S., 7
Bernstein, M. F., 21, 22
Blackburn, R., 105
Black Coaches and Administrators (BCA), 95–96, 97
Blaich, C., 69
Body parts, injuries by, 57, 58
Bohr, L., 35
Bok, D. C., 30
Bowen, H. R., 20, 21, 24, 28, 29
Bowen, W. G., 21, 26, 27, 34, 66, 67, 68, 69, 73
Brand, M., 20, 50, 94, 98
Brooks, D., 94
Brooks R. L., 68, 73
Brown University, Cohen v., 49–50
Brutlag, M. B., 50
Bryant, A. N., 39
Budgeting: advantages/disadvantages of, 15–17; definition, 10–12; practices of U.S. corporations, 13
Budgets: assumptions about, 13–14; definition, 10–12; preparing, 12–13; updating the process, 14–15
Busenberg, B., 97, 98

National Federation of State High Schools Association (NFHS), 48, 61
National Survey of Student Engagement (NSSE), 38–39
NCAA. *See* National Collegiate Athletic Association (NCAA)
New York Times, 25
New Zealand rugby players, 61
Noble, J., 104
Nora, A., 35
Norman, G., 104
Northwestern University, 27

Off-campus groups, 108
Office for Civil Rights (OCR), 44
Office of Postsecondary Education (OPE), 47
O'Hanlon, J., 38
Operating budgets, 10
Orszag, J. N., 5, 27, 28
Orszag, P. R., 5, 27
Ott, M., 106, 107, 109, 110

Palmer, M. M., 35, 38
Participation: equitable opportunities for, 44; high school Federation, 48–49; impact of, 36; rates report, 46–47, 48; school participation frequency, 57
Participative budgeting, 12–13
Pascarella E. T., 35, 36
Paul Robeson Research Center, 95–96
Perceptions, faculty, 106
Performance: academic, 34, 78; college academic, 87–91; high school academic, 83–87; measuring, 16; underperformance, 71–75
Pfeffer, J., 29
Philosophical differences, 67
Physicians, team, 61
PIC (Progress in College), 37
Pless, N., 99
Pole vault, 60
Policies: changes in, 59; extended scope of ISS for, 60–61; prevention, 61; recommendations for, 98–100; statements, 49
Potuto, J. R., 38
Practice: injuries during, 57, 58; policy changes for, 59; pre-season, 59
Practice periods, 59–60
Princeton University, 27
Principles of good practice, 34–35
Privacy, 69
Progress in College (PIC), 37

Proposition 16, 82, 85
Proposition 48, 77, 82, 83–84, 85

Racial diversity and hiring decisions: BCA (Black Coaches and Administrators), 95–96; Black Coaches and Administrators (BCA), 95–96
Raiborn, M., 22, 23, 25
RDMMA (responsible decision-making model for athletics), 50–51
Reclaiming the Game (Bowen and Levin), 66, 68–69
Recruitment, 67–68
Reed, J., 35
Religious values, 39
Reports on equity, 47–48
Representativeness, goal of, 66–68
Research: building on, 68–70; recommendations for future, 28–30, 87–88, 98–100, 99–100
Research organizations, 37–39
Resources: allocation of, 15–16; constraints of, 70; consumption of, 17; gender equity materials, 49; list of, 113–115
Responsible decision-making model for athletics (RDMMA), 50–51
Revenues: by classification of institution, 23; debates about, 19; EADA's definitions, 25; from intercollegiate athletics, 22–23; sources of/spending of, 20–21, 29; understanding of, 28
Revenue theory of cost, 29
Rhoades, G., 30
Richards, S., 35
Ridpath, D., 50, 51
Risk assessment, 87
Risk minimization legislation, 59–60
Rolling (continuous) budgets, 15
Roswal, G., 104, 105
Rugby, 61
Rules (NCAA), 59–60

Sack, A. F., 21
SAGE (Social and Group Experiences), 37
Salancik, G. R., 29
Salaries, 23
SAT scores, 77, 84
Savage, H. J., 21, 22
Schmalz, R., 61
Scholarships, 23
Seasons, injuries by, 55–56, 58
Sellers, R., 37

institutional researchers, who provide campus leaders with objective, trustworthy data about student and institutional performance.
ISBN: 978-04704-99283

IR 140   **Using Financial and Personnel Data in a Changing World for Institutional Research**
Nicolas A. Valcik
This volume of *New Directions for Institutional Research* explores the ways in which financial and human resource data can be used in reporting and analysis. With public sources of revenue stagnating or declining and tuition costs increasing, the need for improved efficiencies in an institution's internal practices has become paramount. An institutional research department can use financial and human resource data to conduct analyses of institutional business practices to forecast costs and identify revenue generation. The chapter authors review the use of personnel, expenditure, and revenue data in the performance of institutional research from several perspectives: the role of organizational theory in data mining efforts, integration of various data sources for effective analyses, methodologies for more efficient faculty compensation benchmarking, the impact of state legislative decisions on revenue streams, and return on investment calculations.
ISBN: 978-04704-68517

IR139   **Conducting Institutional Research in Non-Campus-Based Settings**
Robert K. Toutkoushian, Tod R. Massa
One aspect of the institutional research (IR) profession that has not been well documented is the many ways that this research is carried out beyond the confines of a traditional campus-based IR office. The purpose of this volume of *New Directions for Institutional Research* is to provide readers with insight into some of these alternatives and help expand understanding of the nature of institutional research. The chapters in this volume show how institutional research is being conducted by public university system offices, state higher education coordinating boards, institutional-affiliated research offices, and higher education consultants. Because these entities often do not have ready access to campus-specific data, they must be creative in finding ways to obtain data and information that enable them to provide a value-added function in the field. The chapter authors highlight ways in which these offices acquire and use information for institutional research.
ISBN: 978-04704-12749

IR138   **Legal Applications of Data for Institutional Research**
Andrew L. Luna
This volume of *New Directions for Institutional Research* explores the seemingly incongruent forces of statistical reasoning and the law and sheds some light on how institutional researchers can use the two in a complementary manner to prevent a legal action or to help support the rebuttal of a prima facie case (i.e., one that at first glance presents sufficient evidence for the plaintiff to win the case). Until now, there has been little linkage between the disciplines of law and statistics. While the legal profession uses statistics to support an argument, interpretations of statistical outcomes may not follow scientific reasoning. Similarly, a great piece of statistical theory or a tried-and-true methodology among institutional research professionals may be thrown out of court if it fails to meet the rules of evidence or contradicts current legal standing. The information contained within this volume will benefit institutional research practitioners and contribute to a more frequent dialogue concerning the complexities of statistical science within the legal environment.
ISBN: 978-04703-97619

IR137   **Alternative Perspectives in Institutional Planning**
Terry T. Ishitani
Institutional planning is coming to the fore in higher education as states, the federal government, and the public increasingly demand accountability. Institutional researchers, the data stewards for colleges and universities, are becoming involved in such strategic planning, supporting efforts to strengthen institutional efficiency and effectiveness in policymaking. Researchers find that locating, preparing, and presenting necessary data and information for planners is a challenging exercise. In this volume of *New Directions for Institutional Research*, administrators, consultants, researchers, and scholars provide unique, innovative approaches to that challenge. Some authors introduce program applications and statistical techniques; others share case studies. The variety of perspectives and depths of focus makes this a timely, useful guide for institutional researchers.
ISBN: 978-04703-84534

IR136   **Using Qualitative Methods in Institutional Assessment**
Shaun R. Harper, Samuel D. Museus
This volume of *New Directions for Institutional Research* advocates the broad use of qualitative methods in assessment across American higher education: campus cultures, academic success and retention programs, student experiences and learning, and teaching effectiveness. The chapter authors suggest that responses to demands for increased accountability will be insufficient if researchers continue to rely almost exclusively on statistical analyses to assess institutional effectiveness. Instead, they recommend a variety of qualitative approaches that can produce rich and instructive data to guide institutional decision-making and action. In addition, they dispel common myths and misconceptions regarding the use of qualitative methods in assessment.
ISBN: 978-04702-83615

IR135   **Space: The Final Frontier for Institutional Research**
Nicholas A. Valcik
Facilities information, once a world of precious drawings and laborious calculations, has been transformed by the power of information technology. Blueprints securely locked in cabinets have given way to online systems based on geospatial information systems (GIS). The result is nimble systems adaptable to purposes across administrations, applications that integrate divisions—business, institutional research, student affairs—with shared information. This volume of *New Directions for Institutional Research* delves into this new world of facilities information. The authors show how to gather data and how state and other agencies use it. They discuss the necessity of accurate, accessible information for determining and apportioning indirect costs. They look at its use for student recruitment and retention, and they demonstrate how it can even be used to correlate various classroom attributes with student learning success. With twenty-first-century technology, facilities data is useful far beyond traditional business affairs operations—it has become integral to institutional planning and operation.
ISBN: 978-04702-55254

UNITED STATES POSTAL SERVICE®

Statement of Ownership, Management, and Circulation
(All Periodicals Publications Except Requester Publications)

1. Publication Title	2. Publication Number	3. Filing Date
New Directions for Institutional Research	0 2 7 1 _ 0 5 7 9	10/1/2009

4. Issue Frequency	5. Number of Issues Published Annually	6. Annual Subscription Price
Quarterly	4	$109

7. Complete Mailing Address of Known Office of Publication (Not printer) (Street, city, county, state, and ZIP+4®)

Wiley Subscription Services, Inc. at Jossey-Bass, 989 Market St., San Francisco, CA 94103

Contact Person: Joe Schuman
Telephone (Include area code): 415-782-3232

8. Complete Mailing Address of Headquarters or General Business Office of Publisher (Not printer)

Wiley Subscription Services, Inc., 111 River Street, Hoboken, NJ 07030

9. Full Names and Complete Mailing Addresses of Publisher, Editor, and Managing Editor (Do not leave blank)

Publisher (Name and complete mailing address)

Wiley Subscription Services, Inc., A Wiley Company at San Francisco, 989 Market St., San Francisco, CA 94103-1741

Editor (Name and complete mailing address)

Robert Toutkoushian, Educational Leadership/ Policy Studies Education 4220, Indiana Univ., Bloomington IN 47405

Managing Editor (Name and complete mailing address)

Robert Rosenberg, Wiley Subscriptions Services, Inc., 989 Market Street, San Francisco, CA 94103

10. Owner (Do not leave blank. If the publication is owned by a corporation, give the name and address of the corporation immediately followed by the names and addresses of all stockholders owning or holding 1 percent or more of the total amount of stock. If not owned by a corporation, give the names and addresses of the individual owners. If owned by a partnership or other unincorporated firm, give its name and address as well as those of each individual owner. If the publication is published by a nonprofit organization, give its name and address.)

Full Name	Complete Mailing Address
Wiley Subscription Services	111 River Street, Hoboken, NJ 07030
(see attached list)	

11. Known Bondholders, Mortgagees, and Other Security Holders Owning or Holding 1 Percent or More of Total Amount of Bonds, Mortgages, or Other Securities. If none, check box ☑ None

Full Name	Complete Mailing Address

12. Tax Status (For completion by nonprofit organizations authorized to mail at nonprofit rates) (Check one)
The purpose, function, and nonprofit status of this organization and the exempt status for federal income tax purposes:
- ☐ Has Not Changed During Preceding 12 Months
- ☐ Has Changed During Preceding 12 Months (Publisher must submit explanation of change with this statement)

13. Publication Title	14. Issue Date for Circulation Data Below
New Directions for Institutional Research	Summer 2009

15. Extent and Nature of Circulation		Average No. Copies Each Issue During Preceding 12 Months	No. Copies of Single Issue Published Nearest to Filing Date
a. Total Number of Copies (Net press run)		1590	1541
b. Paid Circulation (By Mail and Outside the Mail)	(1) Mailed Outside-County Paid Subscriptions Stated on PS Form 3541 (Include paid distribution above nominal rate, advertiser's proof copies, and exchange copies)	550	373
	(2) Mailed In-County Paid Subscriptions Stated on PS Form 3541 (Include paid distribution above nominal rate, advertiser's proof copies, and exchange copies)	0	0
	(3) Paid Distribution Outside the Mails Including Sales Through Dealers and Carriers, Street Vendors, Counter Sales, and Other Paid Distribution Outside USPS®	0	0
	(4) Paid Distribution by Other Classes of Mail Through the USPS (e.g. First-Class Mail®)	0	0
c. Total Paid Distribution (Sum of 15b (1), (2), (3), and (4))		550	373
d. Free or Nominal Rate Distribution (By Mail and Outside the Mail)	(1) Free or Nominal Rate Outside-County Copies Included on PS Form 3541	55	56
	(2) Free or Nominal Rate In-County Copies Included on PS Form 3541	0	0
	(3) Free or Nominal Rate Copies Mailed at Other Classes Through the USPS (e.g. First-Class Mail)	0	0
	(4) Free or Nominal Rate Distribution Outside the Mail (Carriers or other means)	0	0
e. Total Free or Nominal Rate Distribution (Sum of 15d (1), (2), (3) and (4))		55	56
f. Total Distribution (Sum of 15c and 15e)		605	429
g. Copies not Distributed (See Instructions to Publishers #4 (page #3))		985	1112
h. Total (Sum of 15f and g)		1590	1541
i. Percent Paid (15c divided by 15f times 100)		91%	86%

16. Publication of Statement of Ownership
☐ If the publication is a general publication, publication of this statement is required. Will be printed in the Winter 2009 issue of this publication. ☐ Publication not required.

17. Signature and Title of Editor, Publisher, Business Manager, or Owner

Susan E. Lewis, VP & Publisher - Periodicals

Date: 10/1/2009

I certify that all information furnished on this form is true and complete. I understand that anyone who furnishes false or misleading information on this form or who omits material or information requested on the form may be subject to criminal sanctions (including fines and imprisonment) and/or civil sanctions (including civil penalties).

Lightning Source UK Ltd.
Milton Keynes UK
UKOW05f1112120517
301045UK00003BA/120/P